THE MISSION IS GROWTH

Paul Gannett

CONTENTS

WAR STORY

THE STARS SHINE BRIGHTLY overhead in the dark Middle Eastern sky. My F-15E Strike Eagle stands out in bold relief against the starry heavens. Right now, it is sitting still and silent. But soon, the mighty war machine, bristling with advanced weaponry, will roar to life, shattering the stillness of the night. I will soon be climbing on my mission to defend the United States of America and its people against our enemies.

I am the Flight Lead for a two-ship of F-15E Strike Eagles. My back-seater is the squadron's Director of Operations, and he is a proven warrior. My wingman and his weapons systems officer are also ready for battle. I put on my combat vest as I have over forty times now and prepare myself for war. The vest is packed with all the essential survival gear we might need, including radios, GPS units, maps, signaling devices, knives, water, survival snack kits, and other items in case of an ejection over hostile territory. I am carrying over fifty pounds of equipment. I grab my helmet and night vision goggles, and pack them in my helmet bag.

The last stop is to grab my side-arm from the arming station. I chamber the 9mm round and harness the weapon in my survival vest along with two extra magazines. Finally, I grab the optional two additional magazines of 5.56mm ammunition. After a Jordanian pilot was tortured to death by ISIS by being burned alive in a cage, we had adapted our seat kits to fit a modified M-4 and two magazines that we can quickly assemble. This way, we are better prepared to defend ourselves on the ground. At a minimum, we might be able to take some of the enemy down with us. The barbaric methods of our enemies had sharpened our fighting spirit.

I have already received my intelligence briefing. Our mission is to provide close air support to ground forces West of Baghdad. After a careful "walk around check," I am sure that my jet is in good condition to fly and that the weapons are correctly armed and wired. I shine my light on the pavement to make sure that there are no foreign objects that might get sucked into the powerful engines. Satisfied that all is well, I prepare to mount the steps into my war machine.

One step remains. I always pause on every flight to say a short prayer for the sortie. "Father, thank you for your goodness. I pray that you keep my two-ship safe today. Please use us for your purposes, guide our bombs to their just targets, and keep them from falling on the innocent. In Jesus' name, Amen."

I climb the jet and settle into the cockpit by "building my nest." When I have optimized the tiny space available, I begin my before-engine start checklist. Receiving the signal that my wingman is also ready, I fire up the two jet engines one at a time. After confirming that the engines and all weapons are powered up and working properly, I check in with "Ops" to make sure our refueling tanker will be on time at the rendezvous point.

After arming my weapons payload, my wingman and I taxi to our positions. I call on Tower frequency, "Strike 01 ready for takeoff." I hear the anticipated reply from the tower, "Strike 01 cleared for take-off contact departure." I push my power up slightly and taxi slowly onto the runway as I reply, "Strike 01 cleared for takeoff, push 4."

As I light the afterburners, my heart thrills afresh to the power of the F-15 as the quiet night is shattered by a sudden and deafening roar.

A glow of bright orange illuminates the runway as the raw thrust of the twin engines settles me back into my seat cushion as I climb into the night skies. I think to myself "It's go time!"

RAW MATERIAL

I was born in a suburb of Washington, D.C., where I had five brothers and one sister. I am the middle child with two older brothers, an older sister, and three younger brothers. My older brother Jack was my best friend growing up, and we were fiercely competitive. With just under two years between us, I was close enough in size to be competitive, but he was still decisively bigger and stronger than I was. We did everything together. We shared the same friends, and we would play football or basketball with them nearly every day. Despite having just a small size advantage, his development and aggressiveness were well beyond mine. Jack also had an attitude!

Jack hated to lose. We were almost never on the same team, so I felt the brunt of his fury when he lost his temper. If things were not going his way, and he saw me celebrate a touchdown or make a face that he could even remotely interpret as smug or pleased with myself, he would squash it mercilessly. Although only slightly smaller, I was no match for his physical aggressiveness. Over the years, Jack has learned to harness his aggressiveness in more productive ways than punishing me on the football field. But I can tell you I learned a lot about humility, at least feigned humility, guarding my facial expressions from my brother to avoid unnecessary physical conflict.

I mentioned we did everything together, even school. That is not to say we went to the same school and were in different classrooms. We actually did school together. My parents recognized that I had a desire to excel, and they could fuel that desire by adding competition with my brother. Although outmatched physically by my older brother, I was able to compete in the classroom. We were part of a unique church school structure that was technically a private school but run more closely as a homeschooling environment. There were never more than ten students in each grade. I quickly advanced through earlier grades because of my interest in learning everything Jack was being taught. By the fourth grade, I was in his class. I like to think I have a unique way of motivating myself to continuous self-improvement, but the truth is, I love competition. I have Jack to thank for this!

The result was that I graduated from High School at age 14 at the top of my three-person graduating class, which naturally included Jack. Being far too young for college, my mom enabled me to "self-study" at home for a year before entering Community College. She purchased recordings of a variety of college-level classes to better prepare me. Although well-intentioned, it was not for me. I needed the classroom, grades, and a competitive environment. The next year, at age fifteen, I started full-time in community college getting rides from Jack to our shared classes since I was too young to get my driver's license. The following year, at the age of seventeen, I completed my Associates Degree as a member of the Honors Academy at Prince George's Community College and was accepted into the United States Air Force Academy (USAFA), being recruited for swimming.

Throughout my childhood, I had an intense desire to prove myself. It may not have seemed obvious, but I was full of insecurities: insecurities that I hated and wanted to overcome, defeat, and master. I spent much of my childhood and early adult life obsessed with overcoming my fears and proving myself "worthy." I wanted to prove my worth to my family, my friends, and myself. I wanted to feel valuable when, deep down, I felt insecure, insignificant, and self-conscious.

I rode my first "roller coaster" when I was about six years old at what is now "Six Flags America" in Largo, Maryland. The ride was shaped like a boat and had a single drop that crashed into a pool of water, splashing eagerly-awaiting onlookers with a deluge of water. I was beaming with pride when I was finally big enough to ride, but as the boat slowly crept over the edge then plunged towards the body of water below, my heart leaped out of my chest, and I was terrified.

I never wanted to feel that way again. I maintained my fear of roller coasters into my teenage years. Even my young childhood girlfriend had the hardest time convincing me at 16 years old to go on the "Superman" roller coaster. Talk about emasculating. It was easy fodder for my siblings to poke fun at.

Soon after September 11, 2001, as a young, energetic teenager, I decided I wanted to serve my country and fight our enemies. It did not take long for me to consider being a fighter pilot, even though I had an intrepid fear of rollercoasters. I thought, "Wow, that would be an amazing job, and I bet I could do that. It's supposed to be really hard, but I can do it." I could serve and do Close Air Support to help the ground troops. My brother Jack had indicated he wanted to join the Army, and my eldest brother had spent a time in the Marine Corps.

Why on Earth would a young kid who is afraid of roller coasters want to be a fighter pilot? I also had a bit of claustrophobia. Few environments confine a person to a smaller place for more time than a fighter pilot cockpit. I think the reason I wanted it so badly was so I could prove to myself, and others, that I could conquer my fears and that I was "worthy."

Everyone has their own experiences that shape them from early childhood into adulthood. In my case, the Air Force was receiving someone with a mindset fraught with pride, insecurity, and desire. I was a fiercely motivated but deeply flawed and fearful teenager. Yet, I was not the first such case that entered the halls of the USAFA. The Air Force would harness and enhance my strengths, expose and improve upon my weaknesses, and create the confident and competent fighter pilot that I would become.

THE CALM BEFORE THE STORM

We pick up the airborne tanker on our radarscope and call "radar contact" to Air Traffic Control to let them know we no longer need a point out to the tanker's location. We make initial radio contact with the tanker, then around 20-25 miles, we call visual looking through our night vision goggles. "Strike 01 visual, switches safe, request to join number One to the boom, number Two to the left wing." You get comfortable judging exactly when to request that the tanker start its turn to rollout 2-3 miles in front of you. The tanker pilots also get better at massaging these turns to expedite the rejoins. We then hold about 50 knots of closure until we get to about a half-mile.

Until now, my wingman has been flying formation off my jet trusting that I will put him in a good position for the rejoin. I clear Two to finish his rejoin to the tanker's left wing while I go straight to the boom to start refueling. I start to slow to control my closure using a constant crosscheck between my instruments and looking through my night vision goggles until I arrive in "pre-contact." I momentarily stabilize about two ship lengths behind the extended boom of the tanker— a KC-135 Stratotanker—and remove my night vision goggles.

"Strike 01 astern, ready." The boomer replies, "Strike 01 cleared to contact."

As I slowly inch forward, aligning my helmet with the tip of the boom and press forward to allow the boom to pass just a couple of feet to the left of my canopy, I hear "10, 5, 3, 2, 1, stabilize," from my weapon systems officer (WSO) in the back seat. As the boom passes out of my field of view, my WSO helps make the contact easier. As the tanker's boom operator, or "boomer," makes contact, I use my lip-light to check our fuel gauge to confirm we are taking on gas.

I will spend the next 5-10 minutes using tiny corrections to try to stay in the perfect position relative to the tanker. At first, this is one of the most difficult things for a pilot to master. It gets easier with time and practice, but weather can still cause even the most experienced fighter pilot to become disoriented, leading to a potentially dangerous situation. I have done my fair share of night tanker rejoins and refueling in bad weather. It is not fun. I can only imagine the grit that WSOs must have, as they sit there without control, trusting me to get it right. Thankfully, the weather is clear at the altitude we are refueling.

This will be the first of two AARs (air-to-air refueling) for our transit, and we will refuel five times for this sortie.

After our second refueling, my wingman and I push our power up to clear off from the tanker toward our target area. As we approach our target area, the Joint Terminal Air Controller (JTAC) relays coordinates to a point of interest and requests we execute a targeting pod scan of the area. We are looking for any nefarious activity. The site is nearly completely devoid of civilians, and at this time of night, any personnel moving in and around the area are almost certainly hostiles.

After some time, we have finally found a target to attack. As I am working through the details of the attack with my weapons systems officer and received final approval for weapons release, an urgent voice came over the radio from the Joint Terminal Air Controller (JTAC). "Strike 01, we have a new tasking for you. We have coalition forces Troops in Contact. You're going to be working with JTAC Yankee. Work with C2 for clearance and transit."

This is a change of plans. Instead of attacking our original targets, there is now a more pressing need. Special Forces Troops are on the ground embedded with Kurdish Peshmerga troops in northern Iraq. These US Special Forces have been serving as advisors and helping to train the native Peshmerga to fight against ISIS. Now they are in trouble.

I have been in the theatre now for nearly four months, but this is my first combat mission where American lives are at risk on the ground below me. We usually have strict guidance to keep our aircraft safely above the max effective altitude of the anti-aircraft artillery systems used by ISIS forces. Having a US pilot go down over ISIS territory is politically unacceptable, especially ever since the Jordanian pilot had been tortured to death. But now with the new urgent needs on the ground, we are authorized to increase our acceptable level of risk to assist our fellow Americans on the ground.

THE BATTLE

I quickly coordinate with Command and Control for clearance and transit. I realize that I will need another aerial refueling at a new location closer to our new target area. As we fly northward, I say another prayer for wisdom and protection for my two-ship formation and for the troops on the ground who are engaged in a life or death struggle with ISIS even as I am thundering toward them.

We check in with JTAC Yankee and are given multiple targets for bomb drops in the area. Initially, these are all BOC (Bomb on Coordinate) releases since there is a thick undercast layer of clouds obscuring our view. We execute a couple of attacks using a variety of GPS-guided bombs, dropping through the weather on targets passed by the JTAC.

As my WSO in the backseat is busy coordinating the attacks with the JTAC, I request permission to execute Yo-Yo ops to the tanker. Yo-Yo ops are when you send one fighter to the tanker at a time so you can provide continuous coverage for the JTAC. At the time, we were required to receive approval from Command and Control to execute Yo-Yo ops since it was considered riskier to operate solo without mutual support. Approval takes forever. I calculate a minimum fuel to start executing Yo-Yo ops and keep querying Command and Control every few minutes for approval. Still nothing.

I know this situation meets the criteria for Yo-Yo ops, so as I hit the minimum fuel to execute, I tell my WSO, "We're just going to do it. They have not told us disapproved, so we are just going to do it. Any problem with that?"

"No problem at all," he responds. Instead of asking, I now declare my intentions to Command and Control, "Strike 01 executing Yo-Yo Ops, number one is switches safe, ready for AAR."

I learned after the sortie that the proper approval was given for Yo-Yo operations in a relatively timely manner but had not been effectively communicated down the chain. Apparently, brass at the CAOC (Combined Air Operations Center) were congratulating each other for how quickly they were able to approve the request and support the warfighter. They may have approved the request, but there was a communication breakdown somewhere along the way. Somehow, that approval never made it to the Air Battle Manager (ABM) with whom I was coordinating. A communication contract had broken down. A good decision was made, but it had no effect. I had to make the decision myself.

Despite not having the expressed authority to make that decision, I felt confident that I could face the music back at base if it were determined I made the wrong one. Having no objection from my Director of Operations did not hurt either. Had it been anyone else, my decision would have been the same, but it felt better knowing he was in complete agreement. I was angry yet relieved when I heard the approval was granted but somehow was never passed to us.

Once I make the decision to leave Two and head to the tanker single ship, C2 gives me a point out to the tanker. He is nowhere near where I coordinated him to be. Despite repeated requests to have them moved to a closer track, Command and Control had allowed them to execute their refueling in their previous track as planned. Apparently, the F-16s for that refueling were a little late, so now the tanker is running behind. They are over eighty miles away, and I need gas. I direct the rejoin to expedite as much as possible and drive the tanker as close as possible to the fight so once we refuel, we can quickly reenter the fight. Meanwhile, my WSO continues to monitor the JTAC frequency and Two's next attack. We finally execute the rejoin, and I am taking gas from the boom while Two completes his target attack. After a few minutes, we hear a new voice come over the radio.

"Any aircraft, any aircraft, this is JTAC 13. I need immediate air support. We are receiving heavy effective fire." The urgency in his voice is unmistakable. This is the JTAC on the ground with the rest of his Special Operations Forces (SOF) Team. There is heavy machine gun fire coupled with shouting in the background. I immediately feel my stomach drop. It is emotional. We need to help…Now!

While I finish taking gas from the tanker, my WSO has already started coordinating with JTAC 13 who is receiving the heavy fire. As soon as my refueling is complete, I dive down toward the fight. Number Two must now come up to refuel, and I am headed into battle with my F-15E Strike Eagle. I carefully choose a flight pattern that gives me the best view of the battlefield and allows my WSO to acquire the target area through our targeting pod. I can get short periods of a clear view from the east looking west under the clouds. In and out of the weather, the fog of war is now fully upon us. I cannot tell you how grateful I am at this moment to have a seasoned weapon systems officer in the back seat.

There is an armored vehicle on the ground moving toward the position occupied by our Special Forces. We are fully aware that with the current situation and the weather, we will have to dive to an altitude that will significantly increase our risk and expose us to anti-aircraft fire and to man-portable air defense systems. If I had my way, I would want to rage in at the height of the tree-tops and faster than the speed of sound to scare the living daylights out of the enemy.

I coordinate an angle of attack that mitigates the risk but allows for effective destruction of the armored vehicle. There is a remotely piloted aircraft (RPA) operating overhead just below our altitude. I had attempted unsuccessfully to coordinate a descent with Command and Control and JTAC Yankee who were monitoring the frequency. They were concerned about the RPA in the area below our altitude, and they were wasting too much time. There is no time to wait for approval. JTAC 13 needs this bomb now! ISIS loved to strap massive amounts of explosives to these vehicles and use them as VBIEDs (Vehicle Borne Improvised Explosive Device).

I quickly locate the RPA using my radar and aggressively dive below his altitude to deconflict. We are on final with clearance to release from JTAC 13 when seconds before dropping our bomb there is a sudden call on the radio from JTAC Yankee for us to abort. I start a hard turn to set up for a re-attack while asking JTAC Yankee for the reason for the abort. JTAC Yankee wanted to deconflict the RPA from our bomb fall line so our bomb could not accidentally hit the RPA.

"You've got to be kidding me. We are below his altitude. It's not a factor, plus it's an RPA," I think to myself while continuing my hard turn to set up for a re-attack. At the same time, we see the armored vehicle take a direct hit from something on the ground. We watch as the enemy combatant in the vehicle hops out and starts to run away. The JTAC on the ground tells us to let the Peshmerga handle him; he had something else for us to focus on.

The forces on the ground are still receiving effective fire from several positions. The JTAC starts to try to talk my WSO on to the locations. About this time, Two finishes up on the tanker and is ready to get back in the fight. I make the decision to stay below the weather to support the JTAC. The previous angle I had from east to west above the weather has diminished as the weather has moved farther east. We are flying well within the max effective altitude and range of enemy Anti-Aircraft Artillery (AAA) and man-portable air-defense systems (MANPADS). I know they have them in the area and have seen them used before. The lower we are flying, the easier it is for them to target us. Furthermore, the white clouds above us make our dark grey silhouette easy to see and track. I want to fly a stable platform for my WSO so he can use the targeting pod most effectively. A stable platform flying low makes for a juicy target for the enemy. This, I think to myself, is where things get sporty. I am going to make the enemy prove it. Prove that we cannot stay here and survive. My team knows the risk. I do not even have to tell my wingman I need him below the weather. Immediately, when he checks back into the fight, he asks to rejoin below the weather with me. We all want to do our part. I am hesitant to put them at risk as well, but they know the risk. They want to do their duty. They are ready to fight. Plus, having mutual support is huge to help mitigate our risk. More eyes looking outside for threats.

As we start to circle the fight below the weather, I set a de-confliction altitude game plan with Two and shift my eyeballs to almost exclusively outside at the fight on the ground. This is by far the largest ISIS offensive I had seen. They are well-coordinated in their attack, and it is intense. Explosions and muzzle flashes are everywhere. We need a new risk mitigation game plan. I have my eyeballs outside, and so does the pilot in Two. If we have a missile from a MANPAD launched at us, we will call for flares and "pop" back into the weather to defeat the IR (Infrared) threat. If we see Anti-Aircraft Artillery (AAA) explosions near us, we will pop into the weather so they can no longer visually track us to aim the AAA. We make it a couple of minutes when I see the puff of smoke from an AAA shot exploding near my jet. I immediately direct a climb selecting max afterburner into the weather. They proved it. I was not happy. It was not because someone was shooting at us; it was because I could no longer support the JTAC as well. I had to move, and it ticked me off. We tell JTAC 13, and I come up with the game plan to move back to the east side and set up a racetrack pattern below the weather, but over friendly territory. This would make it significantly harder for ISIS to target us with AAA while still allowing us to support.

We are about to communicate that plan when the JTAC tells us he will send us coordinates for us to attack. We can execute a west to east run above the weather with very low risk and provide the JTAC with the effects he needs. We perform a simultaneous attack with my wingman so both our 500LB bombs come off the jets and impact within seconds.

"Good effects, good effects, shift fire 200M northwest." Within two minutes, We execute a second attack dropping another 500LB off our jet. "Good effects, good effects." Over the radio, we hear significantly less gunfire and a much different tone from JTAC 13. The JTAC had done an outstanding job with the coordinates, and my WSO shifted the fire perfectly.

JTAC 13 now needs us to get our sensors back in the area of a stationary HUMVEE a few hundred yards from their position. I coordinate to move over friendly held territory before descending below the weather. This time, I leave Two above the weather because I want to use his GBU-54 laser-guided weapon to attack the target, and that weapon needed to be released above the weather due to weapon limitations. The plan is for him to drop it above the weather and for us to "Lase" the weapon in below the weather. We call this technique a "Buddy Guide." It takes teamwork and coordination and comes from repeated practice.

We finish the "Talk-On" and find the target. It is time for the attack. We set up the attack and do the final coordination when JTAC Yankee comes over the radio asking about the attack so he can make sure some other assets are de-conflicted. We do him the courtesy and set up the correct geometry for the drop. We get clearance and are close to dropping when once again we are "aborted" by JTAC Yankee. He claims that the HUMVEE is a Peshmerga vehicle. At this point, we are "bingo" and must return to base. After the fact, we learned that the HUMVEE was indeed a Peshmerga vehicle, but ISIS had stolen it and loaded it with explosives. A Special Forces Sniper was able to kill the driver as it approached the friendly location. Our forces had thwarted several attempts by ISIS to get back to the HUMVEE. They wanted us to destroy it, so it was no longer a threat to them.

I thank God that He answered my prayer that day and we were able to meet our objectives. The team in the air and on the ground managed to thwart a major ISIS offensive, and by the Grace of God all U.S. troops were able to make it out of there alive. Of all the combat sorties I flew on this deployment, this was the most difficult and chaotic sortie of them all.

I think back to that day often. It was frustrating, and it did not go the way I would have liked. I did not receive immediate permission to execute Yo-Yo ops, even though I later learned that it was granted just never communicated to me. My tanker was late. The weather was bad. I made several aborted passes. Could I have done anything better? There certainly are decisions I would make differently today given the clarity I now have, but could I have made a better decision at the time? I wanted to do everything possible to help the troops on the ground, and when I think about that day, I think about the aborted passes. I think about how they needed those bombs, but they did not get them. How could

I get better? How could the whole team grow? Ultimately, we were able to prosecute attacks that helped get them out of there alive, but it easily could have gone a different way. There are so many decisions that fighter pilots must make that have life and death consequences. The stakes are high, so we must hold ourselves to the highest standard.

As you can see, this is not a war story where everything goes perfectly. I hope that you can see a glimpse of the massive amount of preparation, communication, conditioning, training, briefing, and effort that go into just one fighter sortie. While I was in the cockpit flying the F-15E, many other people stood with me, making it all possible. In spite of the most careful planning and preparation, the air war never goes according to the perfect plan. Situations change. The fog of war can confuse even the best and most disciplined. Equipment can fail. Pilots as well as commanders can make errors of judgement. Weather can be unpredictable. But in spite of all these odds, a well-trained fighter pilot endeavors to overcome all difficulties and accomplish his ultimate mission.

This book is written from the perspective of a fighter pilot, but it is not primarily written about pilots or for pilots. It is written to help anyone who has a desire to grow from what he is to what he ought to be. I went from an insecure teenager who was afraid of roller coasters to a confident fighter pilot leading an elite team into battle in less than 10 years. Since then, I have come much further. My goal is to show you how that is possible. My goal is to help you grow.

To do this, I have broken this book into two parts. The next four chapters will examine the foundational character and attitudes that drive the best fighter pilots to success. The remaining chapters will examine the practical steps that lead to victory.

Many of you, as readers, are already experts in your own fields, and you face many challenges and obstacles on a daily basis. It is my hope that this book will pass along some of the most important lessons that I have learned as a fighter pilot that may help you excel in your own areas of expertise. I have been blessed to have mentors, instructors, and commanders who have helped me to grow, and I hope these same lessons can benefit you as you climb onward and upward to success and victory.

PART I

CORE VALUES

VALUES FORM THE BASIS for all true success. Values are distinct from any kind of vision or mission statement, and they are not even goals to achieve. It is not what you want to accomplish; it is who you want to be. Values are what you want the members of your organization or team to embody. They are what you are at your core. What you value affects what you do, how you do it, and most importantly, why you do it. Core values are a way for an organization to formally express what they value. They are meant to serve as a foundation for an organization's culture. Formalizing core values in the form of a fancy slogan is simply not enough. Stating what you value as an organization has little effect on whether the members of that organization actually internalize those values. You need people who agree with and desire to practice those values and leaders who prove the organization is committed to those values.

The United States Air Force has identified three core values of "Integrity first, service before self, and excellence in all we do." This chapter will explore how fighter pilots embody and practice these values and how they have created a culture that is committed to those values.

INTEGRITY FIRST

Integrity is the starting point. It is integral for any organization to thrive. It is non-negotiable…First! The United States Air Force Academy has an honor code that states, "We will not lie, steal, or cheat, nor tolerate among us anyone who does." Adherence to the honor code is a commitment that cadets take seriously, and if found in violation, cadets face severe punishment or dismissal. Personal integrity is important, but it does not go far enough in an organization. There must be a level of trust in each one of your teammates; when they tell you something or say they are going to do something, you know unequivocally that they will do it and do it to the best of their ability. Tolerate nothing less. Communicate your expectation to your team in a clear, unmistakable fashion. It is not a threat; it is a promise you are making to each other. Integrity is the groundwork, the framework, for any successful organization. Integrity is the overarching value for each steely-eyed fighter pilot who relies on one another for survival and the mission's success.

Integrity does not simply mean you are honest. It means that, but a whole lot more. It means you are whole and undivided. A person of integrity is not one way in public, but then something different in private. A person of integrity is concerned with character and the constant struggle that is necessary to maintain integrity in all areas. It is a whole-person concept. Although no individual can maintain perfect integrity, a person of integrity will persistently strive to keep their person whole and trustworthy. Mistakes will be made, but when they are made, a person of integrity will acknowledge and rectify their errors. There is an expectation of integrity in the fighter pilot community, and that expectation inspires confidence. In the community, it is understood.

As a fighter pilot, there was one occasion where my integrity was questioned. It may seem petty to you, and it was, but it had profound relational consequences between the fighter pilots and certain members of leadership. I had transitioned from the F-15E to fly the Air Force's newest fighter, the F-35 Lightning II. I had flown a night surface attack sortie as part of a course to become an F-35 Instructor. It was only the third time I had flown at night in an F-35, but I was responsible for the briefing and debriefing of the entire ten aircraft that flew that night. I was in the middle of debriefing with nine other fighter pilots when there was a knock on the door. As a matter of tradition and courtesy, you never interrupt a fighter pilot debrief unless it is important.

"HAZE (my fighter pilot callsign), did you leave a flashlight and finger light in the jet? They found one in your jet." FOD (Foreign Object Debris) is a real hazard in aircraft. A flashlight, screw, or pencil could become lodged in a flight control surface and cause all sorts of problems for the next pilot. It was a big deal if not identified and removed.

"No, I turned it back into Aircrew Flight Equipment." I was in the habit of checking out equipment from AFE rather than bringing my own flashlights to keep things simple and make sure I had accountability for the items.

"They must have checked the wrong jet," I thought. After the debrief, I was asked again to confirm that this was not my flashlight, as I was shown the flashlight and finger light in question.

"Nope, that's not mine…and who uses those?" I quipped, pointing to the unique form of tiny finger light that would clip onto clothing such as a flight suit zipper. At this point, I was a little annoyed that he asked me twice.

The next morning, I got another call from a different Top 3 (the fighter pilot staffing the operations desk). "Hey HAZE, just want to confirm this flashlight that was found last night is not yours? I keep getting questions about it from all the way up the chain."

"No, it's not mine. I don't know what to tell you. I'm starting to get pretty frustrated. Do people not believe me? Have whoever is asking call me directly."

The Top 3, who was a friend, quickly apologized and explained he was just asked to call me and did not know much about the situation. Fighter pilots know that when another fighter pilot tells them something, they can trust they are telling the truth. That does not mean fighter pilots are never wrong. It means if a fighter pilot tells you something, he believes it to be true. There is an expectation based on trust that they are answering truthfully to the best of their ability.

I had forgotten things in the jet before, everyone has, and I always 'fessed up. It was not a big deal if you recognized your error and worked to fix it. Usually, that involved helping find the eraser that fell off your pencil or recovering a checklist you forgot crammed away in the map container. Then, it was customary to deliver a twelve-pack of their choosing to the maintenance troop who had to delay regular maintenance to assist you in finding the FOD.

What followed was weeks of back and forth between operations and maintenance that culminated with an MX (maintenance) Colonel standing up in front of an auditorium of seasoned fighter pilots and telling us there was a zero percent chance that the flashlight was there prior to me flying that night. He claimed there was no way the maintenance troops could miss it between flights; also, the jet had just been through an extensive MX overhaul, and it was impossible they missed it. He was accusing me of lying without directly saying it. He was wrong. He failed to recognize the extent to which fighter pilots embrace integrity as a core value. He should have known better. He became the laughing-stock of the squadron, and he lost the respect of the fighter pilots. We would affectionately refer to this as "Flashlight Gate," and his remarks would be mocked for years. This was a massive failure of leadership on his part. What's more, I had literal proof that it was not my flashlight. The AFE logs proved I returned the flashlight I checked out that night. Immediately following the auditorium address, I approached my Squadron Commander and said,

"Sir, I don't know what to say. Those aren't mine. I even checked out a flashlight from AFE; you can check the logs."

He quickly cut me off and responded, "HAZE, I don't need to check anything. There's no question in my mind. Don't worry about a thing."

Thankfully, my Squadron Commander knew better. He knew his people, and he reassured me of his confidence. That was leadership.

Later, my Group Commander also pulled me aside to tell me that he had zero doubts that I was being honest, and the flashlight was in there before I ever flew that jet. He apologized and said he did not know the MX Colonel would say those things. He thought he was just going to ask for our help in making sure the cockpits are clear of FOD and safe for us to fly. My commander was a fighter pilot who had confidence in the integrity of his fighter pilots.

My leadership knew that our community squashes any hint of dishonesty or trying to cover up mistakes. Fighter pilots have created a culture in which our debriefs are so focused on getting better that the flight leads running the debriefs often point out their own mistakes more than others'. You cannot improve if you do not acknowledge areas to improve. Fighter pilots recognize they can never eliminate mistakes, but they can help reduce their frequency and magnitude by acknowledging them and addressing them directly.

HONOR SERVICE

Self-sacrifice and servicing the needs of the team is something that should garner praise and admiration from everyone in your organization. I want to be clear: I am not saying you should praise workers who sacrifice everything, including their families, to further their careers and the company's interests. What I am saying is that you should foster a culture that honors giving of yourself for the betterment of others and the mission. This means giving your best, your all, to every aspect of what you do. Servant leadership is the most appropriate way to describe the value of service before self. A servant leader does not serve to satisfy his own self-interests and career ambitions. Rather, a servant leader is concerned with the growth and success of their team members. This is the healthy team culture you want to pursue. Honoring selfless service is a way to recognize the ideal we strive to achieve.

Flying fighter jets is a dangerous business. Anyone who flies fighters long enough will experience some degree of loss. Fighter pilots sacrifice their lives on a regular basis flying some of the most complex war machines the world has ever known. I do not mean stepping onto a commercial airliner and flying from point A to B. I am talking flying intentionally unstable airframes and pushing both the capabilities of the airframe and human body to the envelope of what is possible. This is how we stay ahead of our enemies. This is how we can ensure America remains free. This is how we win!

In recent conflicts, enemy aircraft rarely shoot down our aircraft; yet, every time a Fighter Pilot pushes the throttle up to takeoff, he or she is risking life and limb for country. The threat is real and ever present. Those who have given their lives have given the greatest sacrifice. Every fighter squadron has a time-honored tradition to regularly honor them and remember their sacrifice.

Many fighter squadrons celebrate recently passed fighter pilots with awards in their honor. The Gorillas of the 58th Fighter Squadron (58FS) train the world's greatest Fifth Generation Fighter Aircrew in the F-35. We honor Major Stephen "Cajun" Del Bagno, who died in a training accident in the Nellis Test and Training Complex in 2018. He was an Instructor Pilot in the 58FS before his assignment to the "Thunderbirds" demonstration team at Nellis Air Force Base (AFB). We named an award granted to the student who most embodied Cajun's attribute of being "a good dude." This award was introduced in 2019 at the graduation of our very first Basic Course. The Basic Course features students fresh out of pilot training who have never flown a fighter aircraft before this course. We are teaching them this tradition of honor at the start of their fighter pilot careers. No other award is more meaningful to the instructors or students than the "Cajun Award." Honor those who serve! Honor those who are simply good dudes. Honor those who care about the people around them and want to enhance the lives of those in their organization. Cultivating a culture of honor in your organization will foster unity and cohesion that will translate into performance.

EXPECT EXCELLENCE

Fighter pilots expect excellence. They expect excellence of themselves, and they expect excellence of those they rely on. Excellence is not innate. It takes time, determination, practice, attention to detail, and dedication to continuous improvement.

When I first started flying the F-15E in the Basic Course at Seymour Johnson AFB, most people would call my execution far from "excellent." I remember one of my first Offensive Basic Fighter Maneuvers (OBFM) sorties where we were learning to employ and kill adversary aircraft from a position of advantage. I had lofty intent to quickly cycle through my missile WEZs (Weapons Employment Zone) firing the AIM-120 AMRAAM (Advanced Medium-Range Air-to-Air Missile), then the AIM-9M Sidewinder heat-seeking missile, and then finish it off by gunning my instructor's brains out with my M61A1 20MM Gatling gun that fires 6,000 rounds per minute. I was eager to win…too eager!

Straining under the initial onslaught of G forces—the multiplying effect of gravity on the human body—during my turn circle entry maneuver, I grossly mis-timed my maneuver and failed to fire a single missile. I impatiently entered the turn circle too early and failed to ease off as I pulled the "bandit" or adversary aircraft right to the bottom of my HUD (Heads Up Display). Closing far too aggressively, I switched to guns, then heard, "Ease, ease, REPO, Idle, quarter plane," from my WSO. I had so much closure that I quickly overshot and allowed the bandit to reverse and neutralize the fight. I was pathetic. Does that mean I was failing to be "excellent?"

Every instructor, flight lead, or mentor I have had over my fighter pilot career has made me better. You do not build confidence by patting someone on the back every time they fail and saying, "You're fine just the way you are." Confidence becomes engrained as we fail, learn from our mistakes, and get better. Perfection will never be attained, but that is the goal. If you are not perfect, there is room for growth. Ignoring or sugar-coating mistakes is harmful to someone who desires excellence in all they do. You are robbing them of growth. This does not mean we chastise or belittle; it means we are never satisfied with our performance. No fighter pilot should ever think they are good enough. Fighter pilots continuously push each other to be better.

If you are static, not learning, then you are failing to be excellent even if you are above average. To bring your team to the next level, foster an environment of excellence. If I go to war, I want to have the utmost confidence in the people flying and fighting with me. To have that confidence, I must believe they practice excellence and are not satisfied with "good enough" or even "above average."

There have been numerous times where I have "failed" in my career. We have a saying in the community that "there's no such thing as a perfect sortie." Every sortie, every briefing, every moment is an opportunity to learn and grow. The moment you fail to recognize your need to improve is the moment you give an opening to your opposition and fail to be excellent. Excellence is not simply a measure of ability; it is a mindset. A mindset that says, I will be better, and I will win!

Identifying what values matter most to you and your organization is important for developing the culture you want for your organization. These values should intersect in a way that creates your ideal culture. For fighter pilots, an expectation of integrity must exist, or everything else falls apart. Trust is the bedrock for a cohesive team to be successful in battle. Considering service before self-interest enhances this system of trust because it encourages people to look out for each other and help each other improve. These teams foster a culture that demands excellence both from the individual and the team. The result is a cohesive team committed to excellence through continuous improvement so we can win together. In short, together the core values of integrity, service, and excellence foster a winning culture for fighter pilots.

These core values will be present throughout the rest of this book. In the next three chapters, we will pursue more values and traits that help fighter pilots win. You will notice that these core values are consistent throughout and serve as the foundation for what we do, how we do it, and most importantly, why we do it.

SUMMARY FOR APPLICATION

1. **Integrity First:** Integrity is the bedrock for a healthy culture and will enhance team cohesion and drive performance. The value of integrity cannot be understated. For a team to be effective, they must be able to trust others and know that they are trusted.

2. **Honor Service:** Find those in your organization who provide value to those around them and honor their service. Service is not just about working hard. It is about adding value and pouring into team members. Honor those who genuinely serve the team and are not just in it for themselves.

3. **Expect Excellence:** Excellence is a journey, not a destination. Gain confidence by expecting more of yourself and encouraging your team to do the same. Never sell yourself or your team short by ignoring the opportunity to improve. Become elite by practicing excellence and expect to win.

PERSONAL ACCOUNTABILITY

THE VALUE OF PERSONAL accountability for an individual and organization is crucial. Fighter pilots place personal accountability in high esteem and practice it vigorously as one of their most important values. It perfectly aligns with the Air Force's core values of Integrity, Service, and Excellence. Specifically, the core value of integrity enables personal accountability, which is an absolute requirement to produce the core value of excellence. They are perfectly intertwined and interdependent.

This chapter will focus primarily on the need for the highest level of personal accountability to achieve excellence personally and in the workplace. I did not write this chapter to introduce groundbreaking ideas, but if you can truly embrace the importance of personal accountability and apply it to everything you do, you will grow quickly, and your performance will reflect that growth. Furthermore, if you, as a business leader, successfully build a culture that cherishes personal responsibility, your team will flourish. It will not be easy, but it is worth the time and intentional effort.

Personal accountability is not a natural trait that we are born with. Our innate desire, as children, is to get what we want, when we want it, and not to pay for any of our mistakes. It takes discipline, time, and love to teach a child to take responsibility for their actions. It takes time and encouragement to teach a child to take pride in their work. There is a challenge in getting children to do a good job, not for the reward, but because there is value in excellent performance. It takes discipline to teach them to own their mistakes, to admit when they have done something wrong. Even in the absence of a wrong being committed, children often do not want to admit to what they have done.

For example, when I ask my two-year-old, "Did you poop?" his natural response is "no" whether or not he actually soiled his diaper. There is nothing wrong with him pooping in his diaper. He would not be in any kind of trouble, but it does not matter. His natural answer is denial. It is a powerful self-protection measure that I believe is innate in every human being. Personal accountability must be learned and practiced over time.

When I graduated from the USAFA, I started pilot training at Sheppard AFB, TX. When I would receive criticism for my performance in a flight, my gut reaction was defensive. Thankfully, I had received some good advice from mentors at both the Academy and pilot training: "Never pass up the opportunity to keep your mouth shut." This was something I felt equipped to do. After all, I'd had plenty of practice learning the hard way in my childhood when I would mouth off to my brother. I learned to practice not making excuses for my mistakes even when I thought I had a good one. Instead, I would try to take the feedback or criticism to heart and learn from it.

Feedback, when given correctly, should be welcomed. The person providing the feedback is spending their time and energy to make you better. Over time, you will stop actively thinking about excuses as much since you are not in a pattern of voicing them, and you can focus more on learning and getting better. Free your mind from the need to create excuses, and you will find it much easier to absorb valuable feedback.

There can be valid reasons that an error was made but having a reason for making the error does not abdicate you of responsibility to do better next time. Chapter 10 will address the importance of personal accountability in the debrief and why understanding the reason an error was made is critical to identifying the proper fix. I want to address here the fact that there is a very thin line between reasons and excuses. People will routinely mistake their excuses for reasons. Reasons explain why an error was made. An excuse defends the error. Reasons are helpful. Excuses demonstrate a lack of personal accountability. If I am to err, I would rather err on the side of keeping my mouth shut versus making an excuse.

"What about if I am being wrongfully accused of something? Should I just accept fault for something I didn't do?" Of course not. Reference my story about the flashlights in the cockpit. If I had accepted responsibility for the flashlights, I would have been lying. Admitting fault when none is present is not a sign of personal accountability at all. In fact, it shows a lack of integrity and intestinal fortitude when you admit to something you did not do. The point is to not try to deflect blame or criticism by making excuses. You may genuinely believe someone or something else is more at fault, but if you are always pointing fingers rather than examining what you could do better, you are probably missing out on growth opportunities. When something does not go as planned, or you make mistakes, it is important to own them.

In pilot training, everything you do is evaluated. Every aspect of every flight is graded, and your ranking influences what aircraft you eventually get to fly for potentially the rest of your career. You are being racked and stacked based on raw flying ability and your attitude. If you start making excuses or arguing with an instructor, you will quickly find others forming a negative view of you. Any perception of a lack of personal accountability is a big red flag and something that the instructors will lean into.

Intentional mentorship is the best way to fix this problem. It is easy to demand behavior modification, but what you really need here is character growth. That requires personal, one-on-one mentorship from a respected mentor. Ideally, any instructor can perform this role. When instructors recognize weakness in this area, it becomes the most important thing to improve. Your flying prowess ceases to matter if you have a problem with personal accountability and accepting feedback. When a student is identified as having an "attitude problem," that is nearly always synonymous with a lack of personal responsibility. Simply put, they do not take input well. That is a massive problem because their entire career depends on their ability to accept feedback so they can grow. The problem must be fixed, or the instructors risk delivering a less-than-satisfactory product to the CAF (Combat Air Force).

After pilot training, fighter pilots attend a two-month Introduction to Fighter Fundamentals (IFF) class before moving on to their assigned airframe's Basic Course. Any lingering "attitude problems" from pilot training are quickly and aggressively addressed in the fighter Basic Courses. Someone who lacks personal accountability may be capable of the basics, but anemic growth will inevitably prevent them from becoming the elite performers we need. A less naturally gifted pilot with a strong sense of personal accountability will make a much better fighter pilot in the long run than the most proficient pilot with an attitude problem. Furthermore, a lack of personal accountability will negatively affect the organization's entire culture. In the fighter community, we simply cannot stand for it. You may be the most talented pilot, but if you lack personal accountability, then you have no place in a fighter squadron. It is a part of who we are and has to be for us to grow as individuals and as a team.

Fighter communities demand the highest level of personal accountability. What we do is just too important and too difficult to accept anything less. We count on each other, and our country counts on us. We are entrusted with the power and responsibility to defend our nation, including taking lives, if ever necessary. We must be the best, and being the best requires accountability. We cannot accept those who excuse away every little mistake they make or even those who only hold themselves to a "normal" level of personal accountability.

Most people claim to be personally accountable for their actions. But while those with this average level of personal accountability may admit fault in the face of failure, they then exclaim, "well, all I can do is my best," or "at least I tried." While true, this is too often yet another way of excusing away their responsibility after they have failed; they surrender to mediocrity and lack a desire to discover solutions to their mistakes. This is why I say fighter pilots require extreme personal accountability. Mediocrity and complacency are never an option if you want to win, and we must win.

Personal accountability requires you to face your results with a clear lens. It requires you to face your limitations, learn, and grow. Are you selling yourself short? Is there really nothing else you could do better? You may have done your best, but was it good enough? Can you learn from "your best" this time to make "your best" better next time? Of course, not everything is your fault, but do not be passive. Instead, look for opportunities to improve and grow.

Without the growth that personal accountability brings, one cannot hope to achieve maximum potential. There is no way someone can be elite if they do not practice personal responsibility to hold themselves to the standard of excellence free from external pressures. There will always be external stimuli that adversely affect your performance. There is no doubt about it. No situation or circumstance will ever be presented to you in a perfectly clear way with optimal conditions.

Furthermore, others will make mistakes and contribute to their own failures. Do not use their failings to mitigate your own. That is using them as an excuse. It is an individual's responsibility to perform to their utmost ability despite any obstacle holding them back. What more could you have done to gain better clarification to complete the task? To whom could you have talked? How could you have ensured a better outcome? Were you passively allowing things to slip through the cracks or actively finding the cracks and mending them? These are the questions you should be asking so you can grow, learn, and practice excellence in all you do.

Extreme personal accountability, the kind that makes fighter pilots so good, is about a mindset of complete ownership. A mentality like this sounds like, "I am going to make sure this project is a success; I am not letting anything get in my way. This is my project, and there is nothing that is going to keep me from completing my mission." It is a mindset that requires you to understand the implications of external stimuli and take responsibility for the choices you make from those stimuli. There is no room for apathy. Be very careful not to wait helplessly on someone else to do their job. If it is your team's responsibility to have a successful mission, you must never let a miscommunication, misunderstanding, or simple mistake keep your progress derailed. Errors will happen, but you must always actively pursue ways to fix them and get your mission back on track.

When fighter pilots are assigned a task, they know they are responsible. No one else has any obligation to help unless they reach out and ask for it. If I delegate the targeting of a hostile formation to my number Two, he owns that group. The expectation is that he will handle it. That frees up the rest of the formation to execute other tasks such as targeting their own responsibility or searching for undetected aircraft or surface systems. If he is unable to target because he is having radar problems or does not have enough missiles, that does not abdicate him of his responsibility. That is his group, and he is personally responsible for handling it. Two may exhaust all his options to target the group himself and just simply not be able to do it. He may do "everything he can" but still be unable to fulfill his responsibility. But it remains his responsibility until it can be delegated to another responsible party. If he cannot perform his task, he is liable and thereby accountable to request assistance. Since it is his responsibility to target the group adequately, it is his responsibility to communicate his limitations clearly so that the flight lead can make a decision based on that information. This is a simple example, but it demonstrates that even the number Two flight member, whose general responsibility is to follow the flight lead's direction, must still prioritize personal accountability. Much more is expected of flight leads.

The flight lead is responsible for the execution of his formation of two to four aircraft. He is personally accountable for the performance of his entire team and how he leads their execution. Personal accountability, for the leader, goes beyond self. I am accountable for how I lead my team. If my team fails, then I have failed. Even if my performance is impeccable, I cannot point fingers at my team without considering how I can better lead or prepare them for the mission. When we debrief, my responsibility is to ensure my team will learn, grow, and be better next time. Even after I, as the flight lead, have delegated targeting responsibility to number Two, I am still maintaining awareness of what is happening in that engagement. If Two were to fail in all of his targeting responsibilities and then fail to communicate his inability, the flight lead is still responsible.

In our previous example, there are checkpoints along the engagement where I will check Two's progress in targeting that group and provide assistance if I deem necessary. There are certain things I am expecting to hear and observe along the way. In effect, I am, monitoring Two's actions while simultaneously executing my own responsibilities. This is not micromanagement; this is mutual support. I trust number Two to perform his responsibilities, but personal accountability means that when able, I must continue to monitor the entire situation to make sure nothing gets in the way of my flight's mission success. I am keeping my eyes and ears open to threats to our success. If Two fails, the team fails; therefore, I will do everything I can to make sure he does not fail. If we have mission failure because Number Two failed to target correctly, he will not be the only one at fault. He will be accountable for his mistake, but so will I. As a leader, personal accountability includes not only the actions I take, but also the actions others take that are under my care or responsibility.

Allow me to offer a simple example that I believe is widely relatable. It is my opinion that the courtesy copy (CC) in email is widely abused. People too often use it to relieve themselves of some level of responsibility. "Well, now my boss knows I sent the email. That's all

I can do." Psychologically, this provides a lessening sense of need to follow-up or ensure follow-through. After all, if the task fails at this point, everyone will know the email was sent, and it is not my fault if actions beyond that were not completed. Alternately, the sender might say, "Well, you saw what was going on. If you had any input, you should have said something." This may provide perceived relief from having responsibility or following through with others. I am not saying that the CC function in email does not have value; I think it does. The point is to not fall into the trap of diminishing your personal accountability to complete a task by creating a paper trail. Instead of being used to abdicate responsibility, the CC function should be used to enhance situational awareness and keep leaders appraised of progress. Tools, like the CC function in email, should be used to demonstrate personal accountability through the efficient execution of the mission.

Culture is what makes personal accountability work in any team. Without a culture that treasures personal accountability, personally accountable individuals will find themselves frustrated and potentially begin to lose their own sense of responsibility by the dulling effect of others. A personally responsible person in this culture may end up bearing the brunt of the workload and get upset when others fail to take any responsibility or pride in their work. It is a common experience in many organizations, where a few people end up doing most of the work, while the rest sit back and only do "their part." This is consistent with the Pareto Principle, also known as the law of the vital few. When a manager has someone they can rely on, they tend to lean on them. To the personally accountable, the rest of the team seemingly gets away with not "doing their part." This can be incredibly frustrating for the personally responsible individual as they bear the burden. This may result in the individual failing under the weight or choosing to leave the organization. Both are unfortunate outcomes for an organization. Thus, it is vital to get the culture right. So, where do you start?

The short answer is that you must start with yourself. Everyone needs to work on his or her own personal accountability. Starting with yourself is itself a way of embracing this value of personal responsibility. You are not throwing your hands up in defeat. You are recognizing your part and how you can make things better. Too often, people blame leadership for poor culture and are paralyzed by the belief that they are helpless to effect change. I am not saying leadership is not at fault; we will address how they can affect change next. The reality is there is plenty that can be done in your sphere of influence, no matter where it is. You can help effect change by first embracing a higher level of personal accountability for yourself and then influencing others in your sphere. No matter your position in a culture, you have a sphere of influence. Use it!

I think the most effective way to build this culture is through personal mentorship. I have found that mentorship is infectious. When you receive good mentorship, you want to pass it on. What results is a cycle of personal improvement. Investing in others' lives pays dividends in an organization. Everyone needs it, and everyone can benefit from it. When you mentor, it is crucial to address this area of personal accountability. It is about personal development, and I would argue it is one of the most important ways to help someone achieve more of their potential. Sometimes it takes another person to identify areas that need improvement. Challenge your mentee to see things differently and focus on the betterment of the mentee. In turn, this will challenge you to also focus on your own betterment. You will learn, and as you teach, you will reinforce these concepts for your own growth. What if you can help others reach their potential? The feeling of accomplishment and pride as you pour into others and see their growth is incredibly fulfilling.

Being a mentor does not mean you have all the answers; you need continued growth also. If you are not receiving mentorship, seek it out. Find someone who you trust and practices personal accountability to become excellent in all they do. The person you are looking for does not have to be the best at what they do. They do not need to be formal "leaders." Too often, we consider mentors for our careers. That can be important, but much more important is a mentor for character.

As we will discuss in the next chapter, they simply must be humble, approachable, and credible to help you grow. If you practice personal accountability, mentor someone to be personally accountable, and become a protégé of a personally responsible mentor, you will begin to influence the culture around you.

If you are a leader, you can influence culture change, but it is easier said than done. Imagine two leaders. The first leader loves holding people accountable. When someone makes an error, they are all over them. They even parade their mistake in front of the rest of the team to make an example out of them. This leader likes to keep his own mistakes under wraps, so no one questions his credibility. After all, it is his followers he needs to keep in line; highlighting a mistake he made would only serve to give them an excuse for their own actions—if the leader does not do things right all the time, then why should I? However, whenever he sees a team member openly and regularly admit to making errors, he quickly starts to lose confidence in them. It reinforces the idea that this person is a screwup. Now, imagine a leader who rarely punishes his team for errors. This leader loves the opportunity to learn from mistakes. This leader publicly thanks members of his team for highlighting a mistake and offering solutions to how his team can avoid making that mistake again. This leader always seems to find a way to share in the "blame" when something goes wrong and is intent on making sure his team knows he is fallible and needs to grow. When a member of his team is quick to take responsibility, he is quick to reward them. Which leader do you think is most conducive to a culture of personal accountability? The answer is obvious.

Personal accountability is not natural. Many people live under the illusion that they embrace personal accountability. This is why I call it "normal personal accountability." The truth is most people fail to embrace complete ownership for their actions and instead make excuses or defeatist statements like "well, at least I tried" with no conviction to improve. As with any virtue, personal accountability will take a lifetime of character development to grow and develop, but developing this character trait will pay massive dividends for an individual and organization. When you choose to take complete ownership of your actions, you are taking the first step toward practicing excellence by acknowledging your need to improve. For the leader, this includes taking personal accountability for your team and its mission. If you want your best and your team's best to be a moving target that is ever increasing, then taking complete ownership is the place to start. The character trait of what I call extreme personal accountability inevitably creates growth for the individual. Likewise, an organization whose culture promotes and encourages personal accountability is poised for growth. Organizational culture change is difficult. However, individuals who adopt a personal accountability mindset and challenge others to do the same can begin to create a culture of personal responsibility in their sphere of influence. Consider mentorship as a tool for encouraging and fostering an environment that cherishes personal accountability. In the next chapter, we will discuss additional traits that are necessary to lead and mentor effectively. These are the same traits you are looking for in a mentor that can help you on your quest for growth.

SUMMARY FOR APPLICATION

1. **Personal accountability is difficult, and most people fail:** As humans, we have an innate desire to avoid responsibility for our actions. Most people live under the illusion that they are personally accountable. However, they too often make excuses for their failures or concede with statements like "I did my best" or "at least I tried."

2. **Look for ways to succeed despite failures:** An inward focus on what you can do to ensure success keeps you from blaming others. Never be content with just "doing your part." The only person you have complete control over is yourself. Always ask yourself, "what can I do to make sure we succeed."

3. **Personal accountability leads to growth:** Personal accountability provides a clear lens through which you can see the need to improve and practice excellence. It is more than acknowledging failure; it is about taking full ownership of that failure so they can learn. They are always looking for ways to improve and make their best better.

4. **A culture of personal accountability can start with you.** If you wonder what can be done to create an accountable culture, the answer always begins with you. Whether you are a worker bee or chief executive, you can influence the culture of your organization. Influence others through intentional mentorship to share your value and find a mentor who can help you continue to grow.

HUMBLE LEADERSHIP

The USAF Fighter Weapons School is where the most capable candidates become the world's most elite tactical aviators. Only experienced instructor pilots are welcome to apply, and they must pass substantial scrutiny to be considered for the grueling six-month course designed to take the best fighter pilots to the next level. Not only will the graduates be the tactical experts in their airframe, but they will also learn how to best integrate with other platforms to achieve the mission. The most advanced flying in the world happens here, and tactics are developed at this elite school.

Additionally, and perhaps more importantly, the newly minted "patches" that earn the title of Weapons School Graduate will become the instructors who mold future fighter pilot instructors. At their units, they ensure each instructor pilot student receives training in current tactics and teaches them how to communicate the reason behind the tactics. The patches will be the tactical leaders in their units.

In a typical fighter squadron, the Squadron Commander commands and takes care of the people, the Direct of Operations (DO) runs the day-to-day activities to make the squadron run smoothly, and the "patch" is responsible for the tactical prowess of the unit and the health of its instructors. The patch is responsible for ensuring the whole squadron is on the same page on the latest tactics. He is responsible for prioritizing the threats we train against, how we interpret and apply our tactical manual, and how instructors should build and brief scenarios that meet the training objective. The "patch" ensures that the team is ready for combat.

The best fighter pilots embody certain characteristics that allow them to lead and influence other fighter pilots effectively. The creed of the USAF Weapons School has been disseminated throughout the Fighter Pilot community so that all fighter pilots can strive to embody it. The USAF Weapons School creed is: "Humble, Approachable, Credible." While I am not a Weapons School graduate, I strive to fulfill this creed. I recall when my squadron commander at the 58th FS taught a "Fighter Pilot 101" course to our newest batch of students fresh out of pilot training. As part of his introduction into what was expected of a young fighter pilot, he emphasized these traits are of the utmost importance for each student from this point forward. Without these traits, even the best tactical aviator would be unable to lead their squadron and better the people around them. The people you are trying to lead will either be deprived of the full benefit of your expertise, or they may shun your leadership altogether. If you are absent these virtues, your people will not want to follow you. If you want to maximize your value to the team, be humble, approachable, and credible. This chapter will examine how these three characteristics are vital to individual and team growth.

HUMBLE

What does it mean to be humble? If you were to poll the Air Force on what traits they thought best characterized fighter pilots, I guarantee you it would not include "humble." You are much more likely to hear "cocky," "arrogant," or even "egotistical." Those terms are not entirely wrong. There is a necessary degree of self-confidence to do what we do. Making split-second life and death decisions demands decisiveness; decisiveness requires confidence. Sometimes this self-confidence can translate to a feeling of superiority that leads to arrogance. Fighter pilots are elite, and they know it. Sometimes that manifests itself in unhealthy, unhelpful ways. Humans are deeply flawed, and all have deep-seated insecurities that creep to the surface or, in some cases, spring to the surface. Vices are often perversions of good things. Confidence is a good thing but can quickly be perverted and turn to arrogance. Arrogant people fail to lead because people detect their conceit and do not want to follow. They are too busy being on the defensive, guarding their self-worth against any attack. An attitude of superiority can be toxic to any environment. The Fighter Weapons School recognizes this, which is why humility is first in the creed.

To be effective, a fighter pilot must embody two critical elements of humility. The first is to acknowledge that you do not have all the answers, and you are in dire need of continuous improvement. This may sound familiar to the last two chapters. Humility enables personal accountability, which is foundational for continual improvement resulting in excellence. It is impossible for a fighter pilot to master all aspects of the role; there is just so much to learn. No fighter pilot will ever be complete, lacking nothing.

In chapter two, I said there is no such thing as a perfect sortie. That statement requires acknowledging that every fighter pilot makes mistakes...on every flight! Each time a pilot flies, things happen, and errors occur that necessitate growth through continuous improvement. A fighter pilot may go into a sortie with the expectation they will just "crush it" and not even need a debrief. That expectation is fine and can even be helpful for execution, but after the sortie, if they maintain that mindset, they will fail. They will fail to grow and get better, and they will quickly lose the respect of others and any tactical prowess they thought they had. Conversely, if they humbly recognize their need for continuous improvement and eagerly desire to learn from their mistakes, they will grow and influence others to do the same.

The world of aerial combat, much like the world of business, is constantly changing and becoming more complex. Emerging technologies demand that tactics evolve quickly to keep up. The enemy keeps improving, and so must we. Sometimes tactics that are valid and executable today become irrelevant tomorrow. The ability to adapt is vital. Change is inevitable, and humility is the key to adaptable growth. An effective fighter pilot must be receptive to new ideas to solve problems. Anchoring is dangerous. It takes humility to adapt and recognize that there is a better solution than what you have figured out previously. Some may acknowledge this first element of humility—the need to improve and grow—but still fail to lead because they lack the second element of humility.

The second element of humility is more subtle. It is not as easy to identify, making it somewhat more elusive. I have seen fighter pilots who were outstanding in the jet, exceptional at communicating the what, how, and even why, and even willing to learn from their mistakes. Yet, they failed to lead effectively because they lacked empathy. Empathy is very different from sympathy. Sympathy is a valuable trait for peers, spouses, and friends. Having someone to vent to who can listen and sympathize can help an individual feel better and even promote unity in a team. However, sympathy fails to help the leader solve the problem and encourage a more productive team. Empathy, on the other hand, is vital to get to the root of a problem.

Fighter pilots are not known for having a sympathetic ear. We don't like to hear excuses. We call it "quibbling." We call it quibbling because we value the kind of personal accountability that we talked about in the last chapter. When we see someone making mistake after mistake or failing to measure up to standards, a common tendency is to put more pressure on that person to perform. When a student fails to answer questions correctly in the brief, there can be an assumption that they have not prepared, which means they must not care or do not have a strong work ethic. Maybe they do not have what it takes to be a fighter pilot. Some can even start to form opinions of students based on these assumptions.

The F-15E specializes in deep interdiction. F-15E pilots train to use a low-level ingress to avoid enemy radar detection. This can increase survivability and help achieve mission success with bombs on target. The F-15E is equipped with a navigation pod with terrain-following radar that maps the ground while flying at speeds up to 600knots. This enables low-altitude flight at night under low-illumination where NVGs are less effective. It makes it possible to fly within 100' of the ground while not being able to see any terrain. Trust in the system is difficult to build and only comes with practice and a deep understanding of how it works, its limitations, and how it can kill you. It can and has killed a number of fighter pilots over the years. Even though it is flying the aircraft using a form of autopilot, it requires strict monitoring for any malfunction or deviation from operating limitations. A deviation, if unnoticed, can be deadly. System knowledge must be pristine. If a pilot does not know a limit, it could mean death for him and his WSO. Both crewmembers must be flawless in their understanding. If a student cannot produce the correct answer to a question in the brief, they do not get to fly that day. They will fail before ever getting in the jet. How should a leader deal with a person who is failing to perform?

A prideful person may say, "There must be something wrong with their motivation, or maybe they just don't have what it takes. They should be better than that." Sympathy would concede, "Oh, you're right, it's too hard to study and understand the tactics and memorize all the things we need to memorize. It's fine, I understand." That attitude, while sympathizing, would have disastrous consequences. Unprepared fighter pilots are dangerous. They put themselves and everyone they fly with at increased risk. Empathy rooted in humility digs deeper to understand the crucial "why?" Why is the person failing to perform? What is the root cause? Once you understand why, empathy will lead you to help find a solution. Maybe that solution is rooted in improving the personal accountability of the student.

Humility is a vital trait of someone who is personally accountable. Perhaps you failed to set that person up for success, and she had no idea what to study. There is so much to learn that no fighter pilot could ever know it all. What if she had spent the bulk of her time studying less important facets of the mission? Every situation is different, and every person is different. Empathy allows the instructor or leader to put himself in the shoes of subordinates to find out what they need to be successful! That is the goal: finding out how you can help someone grow so they can perform and provide value. A humble heart recognizes where people are, why they are there, and desires to help them get to where they want or need to be. When you are humbly invested in your team's success, you will find it much easier to acquire the second trait of being approachable.

APPROACHABLE

From the time I started at the Academy, I routinely heard leaders introduce themselves, claiming, "I have an open-door policy." The intent is to communicate openness, availability, and approachability. I have heard this buzz phrase so many times it is almost comical. I almost chuckle at the irony when I walk by offices of these "open-door policy" leaders and see their door closed. I know the message they are trying to send is that they are available, but too often, their promise is empty. The buzz phrase means nothing unless proven to be true.

To lead effectively, you must be approachable. Two vital outcomes can be achieved when you are approachable. First, you will be able to share your vision and expertise more effectively. Second, you will receive valuable feedback and insight that will expand your mind and vision. Every leader wants to be seen as approachable, but not many actually are. Everyone seemingly knows it is important, but how do you demonstrate it?

Fighter pilots are not all approachable. The most effective and valuable ones develop the trait, but certainly not all of them practice true "open-door" policies. I once had a squadron "patch" who was maybe the most talented fighter pilot I had ever met, but he was not always the most approachable. He had his shiny penny favorites, but most students hated flying with him because he always made them feel inadequate. His instruction was always valid and accurate, but his communication created an us-versus-them environment that served to degrade squadron cohesiveness. If you were not part of his "A-Team," you were unlikely to go to him with a question you have about tactics. He possessed value—great value—but he failed to meet his potential during that period. I have faith he will improve and increase his value to the Air Force, but a lack of humility was his obstacle to approachability and put a cap on his value.

A humble disposition is the first step toward approachability and is enhanced through availability and practice. When someone comes to you with a question, are you always busy, or do you make time to help? Availability is massively important because it demonstrates care and creates opportunity to lead. Being approachable does not mean you have to stop everything you are doing, clear your schedule, and be available. However, it does mean you should never dismiss people, whether peers or subordinates, when they come to you for clarification, feedback, or an idea on how to do something better simply because you are too busy. That is unacceptable.

There has to be processes in place to address needs for clarification, feedback, and ideas for improvement. Subordinates may be stuck until they get the one piece of information or clarification they need from you. How can they get it if your open-door policy is just a good intention? Finding time and space to complete a feedback loop is vital. I am not talking about sending out a "culture survey" annually to see what people are feeling. I am talking about a space where feedback can be shared on a regular basis. To be efficient, the feedback has to be near real-time. What is that space in your organization or team? How do you make that happen? It starts with a practice of feedback at all levels.

Most organizations have a "chain of command," even if called by a different name. The factory worker rarely has a direct line to the company's CEO. It is vital that companies encourage their workers at all levels to be approachable and open to feedback. As a Flight Commander, I had about a dozen fighter pilots that I worked closely with and with whom I maintained near-peer relationships. I solicited their feedback often. I would ask them questions like, "what are your goals?" "How do you think you're progressing?" "How do you think your training is going?" "Do you have any qualms with any of the instructors?" "Is there anything you think we could be doing better as a squadron?" These and many other standard questions supervisors should be asking.

I recall having one formal feedback session with each of the members of my flight. This gave me a baseline to work from, but the rest was informal, micro-interactions. I think these micro-interactions are vital. For these interactions to be meaningful, there must be a safe space for feedback. This is where approachability requires trust. They have to trust that you are genuinely concerned with their success. My peer Flight Commanders and I had the ear of the Squadron Commander and could keep him informed of problems in the squadron. We were also the buffer to protect our flight members from perceived bias or an attributional environment. If the Squadron Commander were displeased with a piece of feedback, he would understand that we thought it was valid and should be brought to him. Ensure the risk is low when people entrust you with their feedback, and you will become more approachable.

Perhaps the most effective way to demonstrate approachability is through how you receive feedback. If you receive feedback poorly, everyone from your supervisor to your peers, and especially your subordinates, will notice, and you will prove un-approachable. As a leader, it is a fatal flaw because you will immediately lose all useful feedback sources save one. This is why anonymous feedback is so commonly utilized to encourage honest responses free from fear of retribution. Although anonymous feedback can be useful on occasion, if it is routinely needed, that may be a sign of a lack of approachability. This, once again, points toward a lack of humility coupled with a lack of trust. Being able to solicit and receive meaningful feedback without any fear requires trust that can be earned through micro-interactions that demonstrate humility and prove you approachable. Although the need is readily apparent in leadership, all levels of the organization need this vital trait to be effective.

Creating a culture that encourages approachability and open feedback loops starts with you. Creating a feedback loop free from fear begins with the individual building relationships based on trust. As a leader in the organization, how can you demonstrate how you value feedback without fear? How can you create feedback loops that encourage open and honest dialogue? If you identify shortcomings in this area, what are you doing to fix them? What processes have you set up to make your "open-door policy" actually functional for your organization?

If you are wondering where to start, do not start by soliciting anonymous feedback. Start with the relationship. Speak with your team members directly and openly about how feedback is received, where there are any reservations, and provide a clear expectation that input will always be received with humility and gratitude. After all, the culture you envision for your organization values continuously improving together.

CREDIBLE

An effective team member or team leader must be credible to maximize their value and give people a reason to approach you in the first place. A certain level of expertise is necessary to be credible, but credibility is not just about expertise. It is more about consistently delivering value by being a reliable source for answers and direction. You should desire to be the expert in your field—the one that people come to for answers. This comes with a dedication to staying on the leading edge—that drive to be excellent in everything that you do. If you are trying to lead with no expertise, you are fighting an uphill battle, and the only chance you have is to be seen desperately grasping for that expertise and humbly acknowledging your shortcomings. Even without perfect expertise, you can still have credibility if you can be trusted to give an answer when you have one and humbly knowledge when you are not certain while offering to help discover the solution. Therefore, credibility in the context of the Weapons School creed is about being a reliable resource.

When I entered the F-35 program, the community was still very new. We were trying to figure out how to use this advanced piece of weaponry to its full potential. Upgrades came rapidly, and tactics needed to keep up with the updates. Additionally, we were constantly learning what worked and what did not. We regularly updated tactics based on lessons learned, and there were many. Not to mention, we were trying to open new squadrons and populate hundreds of cockpits with capable fighter pilots. To do this, the USAF needed instructors. To meet this need, the USAF drew experienced fighter pilots from different airframes to quickly transition to the F-35. We had to learn how to fly the most complex war machine ever built, then turn around and instruct others to meet the need for more pilots. In less than a year, I went from knowing next to nothing about this jet to teaching brand new students out of pilot training. I had barely 50 hours in the jet when I instructed my first sortie. Meanwhile, I had nearly 1300 hours in the F-15E and did not complete my instructor upgrade in that jet until I had 1000 hours. I felt underqualified. I was not the only one. The squadron was full of experienced fighter pilots who all had tons of credibility that came with great expertise in their airframes but relatively little expertise in this new jet.

Credibility is a challenge in these situations. We were used to being the experts, and credibility came much more naturally with that expertise. Now, we had to admit, with humility, that we did not know very much at all about this new jet. This became a learning experience that we would figure out together. Becoming credible in this new jet would require dedicated studying and taking advantage of every opportunity to learn and get better. We needed to build expertise quickly so we could become more credible and instruct with confidence the next generation of fighter pilots. We gained credibility through the humble pursuit of knowledge and expertise.

Fighter pilots are taught to be confident and make decisions with conviction. Never be wishy-washy. However, being confidently wrong can massively reduce your credibility. If you are confident enough about something, most people will just go along with it and assume you know what you are talking about. Confidence inspires confidence. This can be very useful at times. When I direct my flight to execute a high-risk tactic to intercept enemy aircraft, I want my voice to carry a confidence that inspires no doubt. I know they will execute whatever tactic I call on the radio because that is how the Air Force trains them. There is no time for a discussion when our 4-ship is closing in on an 8-ship of enemy aircraft that we have to kill to get our strikes to their targets.

Confidence matters, and it keeps my team on task, free from distractions. They do not have to worry; all they have to do is execute. Even if I am not entirely confident it is the best answer or tactic at the time, it is better than being indecisive. It is better than not calling a tactic or continuously changing it last second. That would only confuse, frustrate, and distract my team. If I am wrong in combat, people may die. There are grave consequences for failure, but I must pick the best tactic I can and direct it with conviction. The confidence in my voice will not change whether or not the decision is correct, but it may affect my team's performance. Confidence matters in this case.

If it is training, we can take our time and question whether the decision was the best one in the debrief. It is much easier to examine the best decision when you are at zero knots and one G than when you are hurling towards the enemy with 1500 knots of closure where you do not have the luxury of taking your time. Once on the ground, the quest for the best answer and the best way to solve the problem begins, and it takes humility. This is where being confidently wrong can be so harmful. If my tactic were not the best answer, remaining confidently wrong would negatively impact my credibility. My team would lose trust in my ability to lead them tactically or even lose trust in me as a person. Likewise, if someone asks a question, and I do not know the answer, the worst thing I could do is answer with confidence. Saying, "I don't know," and, "Let's look that up together," is an acceptable answer. Qualifying an answer with, "I think about it this way, but another valid consideration is this," is also appropriate and encourages thoughtfulness. Being confident when you know an answer and humble when you do not will do wonders for your credibility.

The best leaders are humble, approachable, and credible. A humble leader acknowledges his continuous need to improve and demonstrates empathy by meeting people where they are to help them grow. This enables them to practice a real open-door policy where they are genuinely approachable and can effectively lead through trust. Credibility, when the door is truly open, is not simply gained through expertise but a humble pursuit of expertise that builds trust. These traits enable effective leadership that can be truly transformative and create growth in a high-performing organization.

SUMMARY FOR APPLICATION

1. **Humility is absolutely essential for effective leadership:** The first element to humility is the recognition that you do not have all of the answers, and you must continuously improve. The second element of humility needed for leaders is the ability to empathize so you can understand how to help your team meet their potential without jumping to judgmental conclusions about their worth.

2. **Approachability keeps you informed and helps you get the most out of your team:** Embracing the first trait of humility will significantly increase your approachability. The most helpful feedback occurs in a relationship where there is mutual trust and a belief that you are continuously improving together. Set up processes that create the appropriate space to have feedback all the way up the chain that is rooted in trust.

3. **Credibility is about more than just expertise:** Expertise is important to build credibility, but trust is just as important. You want to be trusted to either know the answer or acknowledge when you do not. The quickest way to lose credibility with your team is to pridefully fail to acknowledge when you are wrong, reflecting a

lack of humility or a lack of personal accountability. Credibility is best gained by a humble pursuit of knowledge and expertise.

MEASURED AGGRESSION

*"Fighter pilot is an attitude. It is cockiness. It is aggressiveness.
It is self-confidence. It is a streak of rebelliousness, and it is competitiveness.
But there's something else—there's a spark. There's a desire to be good.
To do well; in the eyes of your peers, and in your own mind." —ROBIN OLDS*

THE FIGHTER PILOT'S MOST valuable asset is his mindset. The attitude that declares, "I will use every ounce of my will to succeed," is what gives him the edge on the battlefield. The belief that "I have what it takes to win" and the creative ingenuity to adapt to an ever-changing landscape enables the fighter pilot to do what no one else can: fly at twice the speed of sound and employ the most highly sophisticated war-fighting machines the world has ever known. It empowers the fighter pilot to make decisions upside down, 90 degrees nose-low, or pulling 9Gs while maintaining the almost super-human situational awareness required to perform our mission and defeat our enemies. This victorious mindset is something that is both innate and learned. There must be a certain seed of this mindset present prior to training, but the training and culture are what cultivate, harness, and enhance the mindset to grow a confident and competent fighter pilot. While we have already discussed much of the fighter pilot mindset from Robin Olds' quote, this chapter will delve deeper into the aggressiveness and competitiveness that propel fighter pilots to victory.

AGGRESSIVENESS: AN INSISTENCE ON WINNING

Fighter Pilots have the reputation of being aggressive, and we are. Aggressiveness often carries negative connotations. Nobody likes a person who is so intent on getting their way that they will belittle, mock, or intimidate others into doing what they want. This is not an uncommon complaint against fighter pilots. Although this criticism is warranted in some cases, it is often a misrepresentation of what is happening. It is not uncommon for a type-A fighter pilot to get frustrated when they interpret others as not holding themselves to the same level of excellence that they expect. Some fighter pilots may lack a degree of emotional intelligence. There are certainly valid reasons for some of the negative feelings toward them. There are also ways that being aggressive fails to serve the fighter pilot while flying.

During pilot training, there is a phase that emphasizes low-level tactical navigation. Toward the end of our training in the T-38 jet trainer, we learned to fly at 500 feet and over 500mph while navigating a route and avoiding hazards such as towers and powerlines that may be a factor that low to the ground. In planning, we map out every hazard and know exactly where every tower is located on our flight route. If we approach a certain distance from one of these towers without acquiring it visually, we climb to a safe altitude 500 feet above the tower.

During one sortie, I was particularly jerky with the flight controls abruptly maneuvering the jet quickly to my safe altitude when necessary. I was probably making my instructor pilot sick in the back seat. During debrief, he criticized me, saying, "You were really aggressive with all of your altitude changes today." I was confused. I had heard Robin Olds' quote and thought that being aggressive was a positive thing. I had a fundamental misunderstanding of how to harness aggression to be positive. It is important that I clarify what it means to have positive aggression.

I cannot remember the first time I heard the term "measured aggression," but it stuck with me over the years. The aggression fighter pilots need to assert is a measured aggression. There must be a compelling reason for everything we do. When we decide to execute, it must be precise, swift, aggressive. The only purpose my jerky stick actuations were achieving was making my instructor hate flying with me. The swift changes were not even helping me get to the correct altitude faster. Because I was being so "aggressive," I would often overshoot my intended altitude and have to correct back with another jerky motion. Conversely, to be aggressive in the fighter pilot sense, I would use precisely the needed input to most efficiently balance speed and control to arrive at my intended destination. No more, no less.

Beyond Visual Range Tactical Intercepts are air-to-air intercepts where the aircraft start at ranges beyond the capabilities of the naked eye, often more than 50 miles apart. When executing these intercepts, there are standard targeting responsibilities based on the location of the friendly four-ship formation in relation to the "picture." The "picture" is a label of the enemy formation from the perspective of the friendly formation. Either the Air Battle Manager or the flight lead makes the picture call. The flight leads are then responsible for ensuring the enemy's destruction while minimizing risk and meeting the mission objectives. The flight lead must direct the tactic, intercept, and targeting for the engagement and then update directives based on constant changes in the dynamic battlefield.

Even before the picture is called, wingmen have an expectation and a responsibility, based on execution standards, of whom they will likely be tasked to kill. They are ready, prepared, and eager to employ their state-of-the-art war machine to destroy the enemy. They cannot wait, pulling like a Pitbull on a leash. At nearly every tactical brief, we reinforce this mentality. "I want you to be a Pitbull on a leash out there. Once I tell you who to kill...that's your kill."

Detailed briefs and countless hours studying tactics shape the minds of these wingmen for battle. They learn aggressiveness; how to execute the tactic. They learn to employ ordnance, and if the bandit maneuvers, communicate that maneuver. Then, if follow-up shots are necessary, based on the briefing, they need to take them without hesitation. They watch the enemy explode and call the kill over the radio to enhance the situational awareness of everyone listening. Then, they look for their next target.

This is what we want from our wingmen, but it is not all we want. We want them to one day become capable flight leads themselves. We want them to be the one who measures and controls the Pitbull. They must progress into the flight lead that makes sure what the Pitbull is doing contributes to the mission's success. Measured aggression is a trait that people learn over time.

Aggressiveness is not about an overbearing attitude. It is about anticipation—staying a step ahead. It is about being ready for what's next and acting with intention to achieve your objectives. To be most effective, you must not be timid. To be timid is to be frozen or reactive. Fighter Pilots must act and act with aggression. Measured aggression empowers the individual or team to lean forward and act with intention and anticipation to keep you ahead of the competition. It combines fierce determination with purpose and direction. This will, in turn, drive elite performance in any individual or organization.

COMPETITION: IRON SHARPENS IRON

Like jet fuel to a thirsty engine, fighter pilots need competition. There is no more competitive act in the world than dogfighting. High Aspect Basic Fighter Maneuvers (HABFM) is when two fighter jets point almost directly at each other and cross at closing speeds well in excess of 1000mph. In this dogfight, both pilots are edging for an advantage. Both are trying to maximize angles while not busting the 500ft bubble, which is a safety measure to avoid a mid-air collision in training. In training, we compete against each other to practice and improve so we can win when faced with an actual enemy aircraft. Each fighter pilot intently looks for cues that manifest in fractions of a second to start their lead-turn and gain a competitive advantage over their adversary. These fleeting cues present opportunities that may afford the ability to get the first shot off. In training, it is the difference between winning and losing; in a combat situation, it is the difference between life and death.

After the initial merge, both fighter pilots violently turn their jets to point back at their adversary while straining to stay conscious under the G-forces. The G-Forces are so intense it requires flexing your lower body and abdominal muscles, utilizing specific breathing techniques, and wearing specialized G-suit equipment just to keep from passing out as blood is drained from your brain by the acceleration. Meanwhile, both pilots struggle to maintain sight of their adversary because to lose it would be devastating. How can you defeat an enemy you cannot even see? How can you optimize your glidepath if you do not even know where you need to go to win?

One of the tenants of dogfighting is "lose sight, lose fight." I want my adversary to lose sight. If I can anticipate my enemy's next move, perhaps I can use some parlor trick to make him lose sight. If I can, it is an easy kill, and I win. The sun can be my best friend to make this happen. If I can maneuver to put myself in the sun, even if it would not be the ideal geometric solution, it may give me enough advantage to win, and in a competition that in combat is life or death, I want to win badly.

Healthy competition is competition rooted in the knowledge that we are all rowing in the same boat in the same direction. Ideally, USAF fighter pilots kill their adversaries well before any visual engagement becomes necessary. We fly as formations, working together to destroy the adversary at range with no losses to our own forces. This is the goal. It is not always possible, though, so we must be ready to dogfight. We have a common purpose; we work together to achieve our goals. We are rowing in the same boat and in the same direction. We compete against each other to make each other better, so our team is better prepared to increase the probability that we all come home alive when the missiles are actually flying in combat. We hold each other to the highest standards because it matters. It matters to them, it matters to me, and it matters to the bombers we are escorting, the troops we are supporting on the ground, and our country that is counting on us to deter our enemies from thinking of attacking our Nation.

When my wingman is better, that is good for me. It makes me safer and makes my country safer. I never want to lose, but if I end up losing in a dogfight in training, I guarantee you, I will humbly learn from that experience and improve. Some of the best learning came on sorties when I was beaten badly. I remember when I was a wingman about to start the flight lead upgrade, I was paired up to dogfight our Wing Commander. He was a 3000+ hour seasoned fighter pilot well-known for his impressive skills. I was an overconfident young fighter pilot who thought I had what it takes to give him a run for his money. I got beat…badly. It was an incredibly humbling experience, and I learned more from that whipping than anytime I had won. I was reminded of my need to continuously improve. He made me better, and I'm grateful.

It is of utmost importance to distinguish between a culture and mindset that is competitive versus cutthroat. It is possible to be rowing in the same boat but lack a common direction. You may be on the same team but desire quite different outcomes. A competitive culture can be incredibly healthy and draw out the best in you and your team. Competition focuses you. It makes you more intent, determined, and purposeful. A competitive environment can sometimes be mistaken as cutthroat. A cutthroat environment is toxic and leads to a culture plagued by bitter, disheartened workers and distasteful leaders. Competition that is unhealthy can tear a team apart. When the competition results in team members desiring different destinations for your boat, it has become unhealthy. Structuring competition in a purposeful manner can catapult an organization toward its goals. Conversely, if an organization's leadership consists of people with an unhealthy sense of competition, the organization itself will struggle to meet its potential.

However, even when competition is structured positively, team members must choose to humbly treasure each other's success.

If I lose in a dogfight in training, and again I hate to lose, it also means my wingman was able to defeat me. That's good! I am glad he or she is on my team, and we are rowing in the boat together toward our common goal of being better fighter pilots to defend our country. This mindset is intentional. It does not just happen. It is easy to fall into the mindset that another person's success means your failure. As deeply flawed human beings, we have natural tendencies to be envious, prideful, and resentful. This mindset is unhealthy and can lead to harmful behaviors that wreck an individual or team. Find ways to make the success or excellence of one team member felt by the rest. This will enhance team cohesion and encourage your team to continue rowing in a shared direction. If you are competitive, that is great! Be intent on making it improve you and the people around you. But be on guard against your own unhealthy sense of competition that may lead to negative aggressiveness and resentment of other people's success. Competition is good, but a cutthroat culture is toxic. Many organizations suffer from an unhealthy competitive culture because of careerists who are there for themselves.

Fighter pilots despise the careerists who will step on anyone's toes just to get ahead. These people are not competitive; they are selfish and toxic. It is usually not hard to identify these people unless you are leadership. For some reason, it is extremely hard for leadership to identify careerists. If it were easy, why do careerists somehow manage to get into leadership roles? When they do, they almost inevitably fail. They fail because they are not respected due to practicing unhealthy competition. They are aggressive about getting what they want, but they fail to make the people around them more effective. They are failing their team while promoting themselves.

Unfortunately, this still happens in the fighter pilot ranks. Every now and then, there is a Squadron Commander or Wing Commander who has been so concerned with "number one" for their whole career that it is difficult for them to lead an effective team because their sense of team is marred. These leaders fail at leading because they have not practiced service before self in the way they compete. They are out of touch with their people and what it takes to create a high-performing organization. They cannot help the team reach its potential because they are focused on themselves and see others as threats to their success. If you want to become a more effective teammate and leader, you must embrace and promote healthy competition while remaining on guard against your own careerist tendencies.

If you find yourself in an organization, whether leading or participating, that is plagued by a culture of unhealthy aggression or competition, then you have a few options. If leading, you can use your influence to create direction for your team, so everyone is rowing in the same direction. An example of this may be establishing incentive structures that reward team performance while still encouraging friendly competition. Additionally, if you are in a role responsible for hiring or promoting talent, consider character equally vital as competency for building your team. This requires considering their reputations for "service before self" among their peers and subordinates since they are often better judges of character than supervisors.

It also calls for asking questions such as "In what ways have you contributed to the success of your team." If answers are always focused on individual accomplishment, it can help you gain a glimpse into what direction they may try to row your boat. If you are not in a position of leadership in your organization that is plagued by a culture of unhealthy aggression or competition, you have two primary options. You can leave that organization and search for one more compatible with your values, or you can focus on using your sphere of influence to lead change. If you choose to stay, you must prepare for a difficult journey fraught with disappointment and challenges to your own character. You may just be able to change the culture from within one relationship at a time, but be prepared for a long struggle. You must be on guard not to allow the toxic culture to infect and mar your own character and values.

Fighter pilots can do incredibly difficult things with precision because of their mindset. A victorious mindset that is intent on winning is rooted in an aggressive attitude that is best refined through competition. Being aggressive means anticipating what is coming next and fiercely executing with conviction. There is no timidity because there is an underlying mindset of confidence and determination that conquers doubt. Aggressive people thrive in competition that is rooted in a knowledge that you are rowing in the same boat and in the same direction. When someone else on your team is successful, you celebrate because it helps you. This kind of competition is not a zero-sum gain. In fact, it is a catalyst for the team's growth through a process meant to optimize the potential of fighter pilots.

These chapters in part 1 have set the foundation of values and mentality that fighter pilots embrace to enable elite performance. In part two, we will examine how fighter pilots tackle complex problems through a process designed to optimize performance and enable continued growth. The purpose is to harness the team's capacity for optimal execution today and then expand their capacity for even better execution in the future. The process starts with building a robust and resilient plan.

SUMMARY FOR APPLICATION

1. **Practice measured aggression.** Measured aggression is about a focused intention on every task necessary to achieve your goal. To be successful in aerial combat and business, it takes a tenacity of mind that is eager to tackle what comes next. Anticipate and act with purpose and conviction.

2. **Healthy competition makes you better, but a cutthroat culture is toxic.** Healthy competition inside a team is rooted in the understanding that you are rowing in the same boat in the same direction. This allows teammates to celebrate each other's successes and grow as a team. Cutthroat competition pits teammates against each other

where the success of one necessitates the failure of the other. This will have disastrous results for team cohesion and performance. Celebrate the success of your teammates and be on guard against careerist tendencies.

PART II

CAREFUL PLANNING

RED FLAG AT NELLIS Air Force Base is the premier realistic training exercise in the Air Force. Integrating the most elite adversary aircraft with a simulated advanced Integrated Air Defense System (IADS) comprised of dozens of Surface-to-Air Missile (SAM) systems creates the most realistic and high-fidelity training in the world. I was the Strike team lead responsible for eight F-15Es, six British GR-4s, and two B-1B Bombers tasked with the primary mission of destroying enemy targets on the ground. At this point in my career, I was an Instructor Pilot in the F-15E and had considerable experience leading similar missions. The Mission Commander (MSN/CC) was an F-22 pilot and friend of mine who was completing his MSN/CC upgrade to make him qualified to lead such forces into combat. His total forces included over 80 airborne aircraft, including F-22 and F-15C planes providing Air-to-Air Escort; F-16, EA-18G, and EC-130 aircraft providing Suppression of Enemy Air Defenses (SEAD); an E-3 AWACS providing Airborne Battle Management; KC-135 refueling tankers; and numerous Space and Cyber entities. He integrated all these assets to meet his Mission Objective of destroying 100 percent of Priority 1 targets and 50% of Priority 2 targets.

The planning for this mission was extensive. My team was tasked with hitting over 60 targets in five target areas. The mission was complex and required intricate planning and integration. I coordinated with the flight leads in my package to develop an out-of-the-box solution to optimize the use of the bombs across our 16 aircraft to ensure mission success. I envisioned maximizing our probability of success by executing a single pass designed to minimize the need to reattack targets by double targeting Priority 1 targets using bombs from separate aircraft. Even if a few of our bombs missed or the planes were shot down prior to releasing their bombs, we were still likely to meet the mission commander's objective.

Normally, missing a target or having a plane shot down before releasing its weapons would trigger a reattack assuming aircraft still had extra bombs to cover the remaining targets. Reattacks often result in aircraft being shot down at increased rates, making mission success even less likely. Reallocating targets to accommodate my plan was no simple task, but my team understood what I was trying to accomplish, and they made it happen. They shuffled loadouts, adjusted formation attack geometry, ran calculations for weapons deliveries, and optimized targeting with a determined mindset. By drastically reducing the probability of a reattack to near zero, we were able to simplify the execution of the plan giving it a higher likelihood of success.

During the three-week exercise, the threat gradually became more and more advanced to challenge the progress and learning of the aircrew. This was the third and final week of the exercise, and the adversaries were unleashed at their highest capability. This was sure to be a challenging mission. The planning paid off! Despite significant fog and friction injected by the adversary by jamming our radar, navigation, and communication systems, we managed to achieve our mission objectives in one pass with no need to reattack. It was one of the most successful missions of the entire exercise. The number of moving parts, all working together with one well-defined objective, was impressive. A plan that remained resilient amid adversity secured the win.

If you listened to the radio that day, it would sound like utter chaos. "Raptor 3 Fox-3 two-ship Bullseye 265-33 25 thousand off Ranch." "Eagle 3 Kill Flanker Bullseye 340-20 19 thousand." "Bone 2 Weapons impact DPIs 1101-1125 successful."

Missions like this will utilize multiple frequencies for different purposes during the mission. In this case, there was an Escort frequency for the air war, a SEAD frequency for attacks against SAM sites, and a Strike frequency for communicating bomb drops and results for tracking mission success and retargeting as required.

The F-15E has three radios and can monitor two of these common frequencies at the same time while maintaining an intra-flight "discrete" radio. This way, I could monitor the Escort frequency to maintain situational awareness on the air picture while simultaneously listening to the Strike frequency. I would be controlling my four-ship flight on the discrete frequency, directing my team of 16 aircraft on the Strike frequency, and coordinating with the Escort Team Lead and his F-22s and F-15Cs on the Escort frequency. Communications were constant with multiple radio calls happening simultaneously. Therefore, it was vital to split volumes in your headset by panning audio left or right to distinguish what call is coming across on what radio. Then predictably, music would blare over one of the frequencies as the adversaries hijacked our frequency and replaced our communications with either propaganda like "you will all die, you capitalist pigs," or some old Beetles music. This would necessitate a coordinated "chattermark" of the entire package to switch to a pre-planned backup frequency. It would seem like complete chaos, but our plan was resilient.

Young fighter pilots have a steep learning curve to be able to process what's happening. They're often just hanging on and trying to maintain visual and doing exactly what their flight leads say. In a few short years, however, they will be leading these missions. So we need them to squeeze every ounce of learning from the plan, brief, execute, debrief cycle so they can handle a little more each flight and become the fighter pilots and leaders we need. We need them to grow!

The process of synchronizing all the different assets and capabilities and using them for a directed purpose is a large part of what makes the Air Force so effective. Fighter pilots continuously update tactics and find creative new ways to integrate new capabilities against a dynamic threat. However, the planning process they use remains largely unchanged. Minor tweaks have been made over time, but it is a tried-and-true way to approach complex problems and tackle them as a team. The process works incredibly well for fighter pilots, but any team on a mission can use them. The distinct, repeatable framework enables you to aggregate a vast number of complex variables and formulate a coherent plan that can be executed with precision. The following six-step planning process can be applied universally in any field to optimize human performance.

STEP 1 – DEFINE THE MISSION OBJECTIVES AND DESIRED EFFECTS: WHAT DOES SUCCESS LOOK LIKE?

Fighter pilots like to work problems starting with the target and working backward. You want to "begin with the end." This works when planning a target attack, but it also works as a framework for an entire mission or strategy. It is of paramount importance that all team members clearly understand the purpose of the task. Everyone has to be on the same page on why we are planning and executing this mission in the first place. What are we trying to accomplish? What is the commander's intent? We are being asked to hit these targets, but why? What are the desired effects, and is there a better way to meet the objective?

It starts with an overall intent. For example, an overall intent may be to gain and maintain air superiority and severely cripple the enemies Command and Control and Counter-Air capabilities to enable follow-on missions. The mission commander can then take this overall intent and break it down into mission objectives. The mission objectives are the mission commander's way of boiling down the overall intent of the mission to measurable, attainable goals that everyone on the team can identify and understand. For a mission objective to be valid, achieving it must provide the effect necessary to meet the overall intent of the mission. Achievement of the mission objectives defines mission success for the team.

The mission commander's responsibility, with input from his team leads, is to establish a valid mission objective. Once the mission objective is set, every action in the plan is developed and analyzed to determine if it is helping to meet the mission objective. If it is not helping achieve those objectives, then it is not worth doing. If it's not helping you meet your mission objective and thereby be successful, don't do it. Distilling this further for individual teams within your larger team will provide the clarification your team needs to solve the problem creatively.

Each team lead uses the mission objectives to create their own tactical objectives for their team. These tactical objectives must meet the same criteria for being measurable and attainable, and by definition, they must help achieve the overall mission objectives. Tactical objectives provide direction and purpose for individual teams searching for creative solutions to accomplish mission success. Both the mission and tactical objectives will be constantly revisited throughout the mission cycle as it flows from the Plan, Brief, Execution, and concludes with the Debrief.

Leaders need to be able to communicate how much risk they are willing to accept to achieve the mission objectives. We call this the Acceptable Level of Risk (ALR), and it changes for each mission based on the overall intent. ALR needs to be considered throughout the mission because it reframes the mission in terms of the overall intent. Once mission objectives are established, there is a tendency to become so focused on accomplishing those objectives that excessive risk can be taken.

In planning a mission, leaders must know how many losses they are willing to accept to achieve a goal. Is the commander willing to accept upwards of 50 percent losses to take out these targets? Is it worth it? If there are multiple objectives, there may be differing amounts of risk acceptable for each objective. Additionally, there will often be a floating level of risk during a mission. At certain points in the mission, we may be unwilling to accept nearly any risk, but other times it may be much higher. These are determinations that must be made by leadership who is tasking the mission, and clearly communicated by the mission commander who is leading the planning and execution of the mission. With clear guidance, the team knows how to plan and execute to accomplish the mission objectives and meet the overall intent.

STEP 2 – CLEARLY DEFINE THE PROBLEM: WHAT ARE YOUR SITUATION AND BARRIERS?

Once the desired effects of the mission are clearly stated, the next step is to clearly identify the environment where you are operating. For a fighter pilot's mission, this would include things like the current political and military situation as well as the weather and physical environmental factors. I like to think of the political and military situation as the strategic environment, and the weather and physical environmental factors as the tactical environment. It is critical to start with the strategic environment to frame the mission and inform decisions throughout the process. The Air Force leverages its intelligence resources to identify the strategic environmental factors.

When I was flying missions into Iraq and Syria, the Russians had just started building up their presence in Syria, and there were Su-30 and Su-35 Flankers flying in theatre. The jets we had been training to defeat for our entire careers would now be flying in the same airspace. So it was imperative to us that we understood their intentions. Why are they there? What will their posture be towards US aircraft in the area? What conversations are being had at the highest level to ensure some kind of understanding and reduce the risk of conflict? How would they interpret our presence, and how should we interpret theirs? We relied on intelligence briefings to update us regularly with the most current political and military situation.

The first several months were awfully testy as we tried to feel each other out while still trying to accomplish our mission of eradicating ISIS from the region. We would try to maintain a position of advantage or, at a minimum, mutual support so that if they tried to shoot down one of our aircraft, there would be immediate consequences. We had to maintain a defensive stance while avoiding escalating the situation or appearing threatening. This landscape was constantly changing. When Turkey shot down a Su-24 for encroaching on its sovereign borders, it increased our risk significantly. Flying in close proximity to Russian fighters was a tense situation. A misunderstanding could result in missiles being fired, generating massive consequences on diplomacy.

The strategic landscape was constantly changing, and agility was key. We had to constantly assess the latest development. What intercepts/encounters happened this week, and what is the intel assessment given all the factors? Understanding and communicating the strategic environment to your team is vital to maintaining the edge and empowering your people to make informed decisions at the tactical level. Who on your team is responsible for updating your team on the strategic environment?

Weather is one of the important tactical environment considerations for fighter pilots. There are so many tactical implications it is hard to exaggerate its importance. A fighter pilot is concerned with where the clouds are; at what altitude the contrails begin and end; what the winds are at altitude and at the surface; where the sun will be during the mission; if it is a night mission, how much moon illumination will be there; and what the humidity is. I cannot possibly go into all the implications of weather on a mission. The impacts are massive, and you have zero control. You can only control how you plan and execute within that environment. These factors must be incorporated in the plan. To ignore them would be a grave error and could result in mission failure. You must understand the environmental factors you can use to your advantage and what factors may pose a problem or roadblock to accomplishing the mission. No matter your tactical environment, understanding it helps you frame the problem more clearly.

The next part of the problem is the enemy. We often say, "The enemy has a vote too." The enemy always has objectives, methods, strengths, and weaknesses, just like us. Just as we rely on intelligence resources to understand the strategic environment, we rely on those same resources to identify and brief the threats. To understand the threat, you must identify both their technical capabilities and their tactics. I must know my enemy better than they know me. Intelligence is key!

For example, for an adversary fighter aircraft threat, I need to know what radar they are carrying, what loadout they generally employ, what electronic attack or protection measures they have, and what tactics we have observed them using in training. Additionally, intel will assess a Most Likely Course of Action (MLCOA) and a Most Dangerous Course of Action (MDCOA). Based on all the intelligence, what is our expectation of the enemy in this mission? Also, what would be the most dangerous response from the enemy? These are vital for developing our game plan to be optimal against the MLCOA while still viable if we encounter the MDCOA.

In civilian life, you may not have an enemy to know and fight in the same way as fighter pilots. However, there is still a most likely and most dangerous path of resistance to whatever you're attempting to accomplish. The barriers to your success are threats to be defeated. Whatever the threat, it is vital that you are informed and know the MLCOA and the MDCOA so you can clearly define the problem.

STEP 3 – IDENTIFY YOUR RESOURCES: WHO IS ON YOUR TEAM, AND WHAT CAN THEY DO?

Once the problem is clearly defined, it is time to inventory what assets are available for the mission, what capability they provide, and how you can best integrate and coordinate those capabilities to achieve the desired effect. Simply, who is on your team, and what can they do? We've identified the enemy's strengths and weaknesses, so now we must position our assets to mitigate their strengths while exploiting their weaknesses. Likewise, we want to build a plan to accentuate our strengths and mask our weaknesses.

I have often been asked how I liked flying the F-35 and how it compares to the F-15E. I have also been asked how these jets matched up against the F-16, F-18, and F-22. Although you can make some comparisons, they each bring something different to the fight. F-15E aircrews often boast that they can do it all. The jet does Air-to-Air really well with its APG-82 Radar and robust weapons loadout and can carry nearly every Air-to-Ground munition in the Air Force inventory. They can fight their way in, drop bombs, and fight their way out. It's a true multi-role fighter. However, never in a million years would we send F-15Es alone and unafraid into battle against a near-peer threat like Russia or China. It would be a blood bath. The same is true for the F-35 or any of our other airframes. Although they may do many different things well, you must consider the highest and best purpose for that asset. F-35s are excellent at a lot of things, but they can't do it all at the same time. You must consider the best use for its capabilities in a given scenario considering the other available assets.

For example, the F-35 can carry and employ 2000lb Joint Direct Attack Munitions (JDAM) and could be used as a primary strike asset. It is excellent at this mission, and there are certainly times it is the best asset to execute this mission. However, F-15Es can also carry JDAMs and more. It may make more sense to take advantage of the F-35s unique ability to find and kill Surface to Air Missile (SAM) systems that may turn on and try to shoot down our aircraft. Instead of pairing their 2000lb bombs against a known target, it makes a whole lot more sense to optimize their loadout and capabilities for finding and killing these elusive and dangerous threats and leave the known targets to the F-15Es. The F-15Es likewise could load up their jets with eight missiles and execute the Escort mission, but it makes a whole lot more sense to leave that mission to the F-22s that enjoy the significant advantage of Stealth in the Air-to-Air fight. F-22s could drop bombs if we needed them to, but they would have to carry fewer missiles to do it. If someone else can do the bomb-dropping job, we could all benefit from the F-22 having an extra couple of missiles. There has to be a prioritization of capabilities for each asset. I want all their capabilities working synergistically to overwhelm the enemy's defenses.

There are so many supporting casts in this play that the idea of trying to "go it alone" is insanity. Every mission is unique, and depending on the desired effect, it will require different resources. These resources include things like fighter aircraft, bombers, refueling tankers, combat search and rescue aircraft, airborne command and control, Intelligence Surveillance, and Reconnaissance (ISR) aircraft to gather intelligence on the battlefield environment, airborne electronic warfare aircraft, space, and cyber warfare assets. This is just a small list of the potential resources the Air Force may employ on a given mission. Various other Naval, Marine Corps, and Army assets may also join these assets. The key is to inventory what capabilities you have to achieve a given effect. What effect do you need? Now, what asset can achieve that effect? Are there any effects we cannot achieve?

Economics is the study of the application of limited resources. Every company encounters scarcity at varying levels. When a company tasks a division with the objective of 25% revenue growth, it is important for the division leaders to know what it needs to accomplish that objective. First, what are the barriers that may prevent us from achieving that objective? This could be competition threatening market share, regulatory obstacles, lack of client education, etc. Do I have the manpower and talent necessary to overcome these threats to achieving the objective? What about financial resources to perform capital improvements or execute a targeted marketing campaign? When there is a shortfall identified, is there a way to request additional resources?

Once you have the list of assets and capabilities, you must answer the question, "Is it sufficient to achieve the mission objectives and thereby satisfy the overall intent?" Will you be able to achieve the desired effect within the given acceptable level of risk? If the answer is no, you must make one of three decisions. One, choose to accept a higher level of risk to achieve the effect. Two, reduce the effect we are trying to achieve until it is back within the acceptable risk. Three, ask for more forces or resources. Perhaps all that is needed is one more asset to significantly reduce our risk. Once you answer these questions, you can then begin planning the mission using a framework for victory.

STEP 4 – PROVIDE A FRAMEWORK FOR VICTORY: DEVELOP AND REFINE USING TEAM LEADERS

The planning process is most efficient when the team leader is able to provide a rough framework for tackling the problem. We call this the "80 percent solution." Your team's time is valuable and limited, so you want to make sure you provide them adequate direction when it is time to plan. Ideally, the leader already has a rough idea of how to tackle the problem and what information he needs from each team leader to validate that solution. This does not mean he has it all figured out. It simply means there is a framework and common vector for the team to begin planning. This framework for solving the problem often includes some form of phased approach to executing each step of the mission. The mission commander will present this initial framework to his team leads and use their expertise to refine it. The mission commander may have a general understanding of what capabilities each team brings to the fight, but he will need significant input from team leads.

Team leaders are responsible for specific mission subsets that directly support the overall mission. For example, an "Escort" team lead is responsible for providing Air-to-Air protection for the entire package. The "SEAD" team lead is responsible for protecting the package from surface threats. The "Strike" team lead is responsible for the plan to destroy targets assigned in the mission with the air-to-ground (A/G) munitions available across the package. The list of team leads covers many other domains, including Space, C2, Tanker, Intel, and Cyber. These experts are responsible for working with the mission commander to devise and refine his plan. If they identify a capability they can provide that will help achieve the mission, but it is not part of the initial "hack" of the plan, they will work with the mission commander to incorporate that capability.

In essence, the team leaders are responsible for optimizing the mission commander's plan and leveraging available capabilities to accomplish the mission. They help the mission commander refine his answer to the questions, "Can we win with the current assets?" and "Can we execute within the acceptable level of risk?" These team leaders support each other to achieve the mission objectives. Often, the whole mission centers on the "strikers" reaching their targets and achieving weapons effects. Everything revolves around getting the strikers to their release points and back out of the threat area. Where are they vulnerable? It all starts with the target.

In business, the application is similar. For example, consider when a restructuring is necessary for a company to make significant changes to its operational structure. A leader must start with the target. What do I want to accomplish with the restructuring? What do I think that would look like? What consequences am I willing to accept to achieve this target structure? This establishes the objective and the acceptable level of risk to get there. Then, the leader must clearly communicate the vision by creating a framework for how it may proceed. Team leaders then take this framework and refine it. Sometimes, this means tearing that framework apart or educating their leader on additional risk factors or costs that may exceed what the leader was willing to accept. This is where humility is vital for the leader. The leader must have established a relationship of trust with team leaders that encourages them to provide direct feedback and speak plainly. He may be right that a new structure is required, but that is not enough. Companies often go through these restructurings only to find the new structure to be just as problematic as the first. They waste time, effort, and resources only to find themselves in a new structure that is equally dysfunctional. In most cases, there were probably team leaders who saw it coming, but failed to act either out of fear of offending the leader or they were never solicited for their help to begin with. Refining the framework using the expertise of team leaders is a critical step that should not be bypassed whenever practical. Once the framework has been set and refined using the expertise of the team leads, you can move on to ensuring roles and responsibilities are clearly understood by the entire team. This requires clear contracts and contingency plans.

STEP 5 – CREATE CLEAR CONTRACTS AND PLAN FOR CONTINGENCIES

Contracts are vital for keeping everyone on the same page, so there is a clear expectation of what should happen and when. At every Red Flag exercise or other major exercise, mission failures often come down to either a lack of or ill-defined contracts that individuals and teams did not understand or follow. Contracts are a way of quickly getting different players on the same page, so there is clearly defined responsibility. Think of them as a "promise" to execute a certain way or provide critical information in a usable way. Ideally, our tactical standards will drive most of our actions and limit the need for additional contracts. Unnecessary contracts overcomplicate missions. Furthermore, they can divert attention away from the mission-essential contracts. It is vital that teams only create contracts if there is a need to deviate from well-established standards. It does not add value to the mission to take what is already in established standards and turn them into contracts. That just makes the mission more complex.

Every contract has a defined approval authority to determine who has the ability to identify the criteria have been met and call for the appropriate action. In some cases, the authority may rest only in the commander. In others, it may be a team lead or simply the first person to recognize the criteria have been met. Then, whoever has the authority must communicate that the contract trigger has been identified. How will it sound, and what is the communication platform that will be used? Finally, when the appropriate communication has taken place, what is the action? Who is responsible for doing what? Again, execution contracts are promises that have structure, so there are clear expectations across the team. Like the rest of the plan, contracts must be tested and incorporate contingencies.

Contingencies are perhaps the most critical part of the planning process. What if things don't go the way we expect? What if the adversary does something unpredicted? What if there are maintenance issues resulting in fewer jets than we anticipated? What if one of our tankers break? How are we going to prioritize the fuel we do have? What if one of our bombs fails to explode, and we need to reattack? What if a SAM system pops up right over our target area? What if my radar, targeting pod, or any of my other sensors stop working? What if one of us is shot down, and we have pilots parachuting into unfriendly territory? What if, what if, what if?

Contingencies are not just things to consider at the end of the planning process. As soon as there is a plan framework and general game plan, we start to consider contingency plans. It is a way of testing our plan to begin with. If our plan cannot easily adapt to contingencies, it is not resilient. The more contingencies that your base plan can handle, the better. Then, for the eventualities your primary plan is not built to handle, you must address a change that occurs if you encounter those situations. How will we adjust in real-time if we encounter one of these contingencies? Often, these contingencies will change the plan enough to generate a contract.

For example, if the plan was to push four F-22s on an initial Air-to-Air Sweep, but only two F-22s make it to the fight due to maintenance issues, then can we still achieve the mission inside our ALR constraints? To do so, it may require adjusting the plan slightly to accommodate this contingency. Perhaps we need some other assets to assist with the Air-to-Air Sweep. It is much easier to think through these contingencies in planning before the mission versus during execution. Execution is not the time to be surprised and have to react. Unfortunately, not all contingencies can possibly be considered in planning. Instead, you should focus on the most likely and most dangerous contingencies, as we discussed earlier. Once you have a well-developed plan, it is time to practice.

STEP 6 – ROCK-DRILL CONTRACTS AND CONTINGENCIES

Rock-drilling contracts and contingencies are essential parts of the planning process to find holes in the game plan. Rock drilling is a dress rehearsal of the plan for the purpose of finding and filling the holes before the plan is finalized. If someone is unclear on what their role is or how to execute it at any point during the exercise, you have found a hole. It is a way of making sure everyone on the team has the same expectation and understanding of the plan. You may also discover that someone is unable to do something you are expecting of them. For example, your C2 team lead may have planned to send a tasking to Strike 1 using a medium that Strike 1 was unable to receive based on platform limitations. The rock-drill would expose this potentially fatal flaw in the plan.

You do not want the mission brief, which we will discuss next chapter, to be the first time you discover there was a misunderstanding amongst the team leaders, and someone was planning something you did not expect. At that point, it's too late to change effectively. However, executing a rock-drill during planning for every contract and contingency will do wonders to refine your plan and prepare your team for success.

COMBATING INDECISION IN PLANNING

> "A good plan, violently executed now,
> is better than a perfect plan next week."
> —GENERAL GEORGE S. PATTON

I love this well-known quote by one of the most renowned generals in American history. It is simple, yet it speaks volumes. I'm guessing you have heard the expression, "analysis paralysis." Some personalities are prone to spontaneous action with little preparation, while others may feel the need to analyze a situation to the nth degree, seemingly taking forever to get anything done. Some act too quickly, while others become paralyzed by their need to get everything right. Some are "all thrust, no vector," while others want the perfect vector and never have any thrust. Patton addressed "analysis paralysis" while also recognizing that it does take a good plan. You cannot just execute violently; you have to execute a good plan violently. It's about balance.

Clarity is hard to come by in combat and in business. I have never executed a perfect plan. There have always been holes in the plan. You try to plug as many holes in the planning process as possible, but there will always be ways to improve. Do not delay execution until you have the perfect plan, or you will never execute anything. As long as it is a good plan, you may benefit far more from a timely execution than waiting for a more perfect plan. I define "good" as giving you an acceptable probability of meeting your mission objectives under your acceptable level of risk. You want to make it as good as possible without sacrificing the initiative or tactical advantage. I will talk more about taking advantage of opportunities violently during the execution portion, but the concept applies in planning. Executing a plan that sets you up for failure is fool hearty, but so is waiting for the perfect plan and letting opportunity slip away.

The basics of mission planning are universal and can make any plan more resilient and likely to succeed. First, you have to define what you want to achieve by answering the question "what does success look like" and clearly communicate that overall intent with mission objectives. Next, you must consider the environment you are operating in and identify barriers to your success. With the desired end-state and problem clearly identified, you can inventory what resources you have available to accomplish your objectives and highlight any shortfalls in your capabilities that need to be addressed. This will allow you to provide a framework for victory and leverage team leaders' expertise to refine that plan. Spend special attention to contracts and contingencies during the entire planning process ensuring they are clear and executable. Once you have fully developed your contracts and contingencies, practice them in a "rock-drill" to allow you to find and fill holes in your plan. Once your good plan is complete, it is time to get the entire team on the same page for execution with a quality brief, which is the focus of the next chapter.

SUMMARY FOR APPLICATION (THE SIX STEPS)

- **Step 1 – Define the Mission Objectives and Desired Effects:** Answering the question, "What does success look like?" sets the tone and direction for your team. Clearly stating the desired end state and the acceptable level of risk sets the foundation for a successful planning process.

- **Step 2 – Clearly Define the Problem:** Knowing the barriers to success and potential pitfalls along the way will help you construct your plan to be resilient. To reach your desired end state, you must navigate these barriers and pitfalls.

- **Step 3 – Identify your Resources:** Answering the question, "Who's on your team and what can they do?" will influence how you tackle the problem presented to you. Now you can start to construct a plan to answer the question of whether you can achieve your objective within the acceptable level of risk. If you cannot, you either need more resources or must accept more risk.

- **Step 4 – Provide a Framework for Victory and Refine Using Team Leaders:** The mission commander needs to use team leaders to help design a framework for victory. Creating a plan framework using phases helps frame the problem at distinct intervals and enables creative problem solving by members of the team.

- **Step 5 – Formalize contracts and plan for contingencies:** Contracts between teams on a mission need to be clearly stated and formalized. These contracts are important for overall mission success and emphasize that importance for execution. Contingency planning makes your plan more resilient when circumstances change. Spend time on the contingencies that are most probable and have the greatest impact on the objective.

- **Step 6 – "Rock-drill" contracts and contingencies:** Practicing how to enact and execute a contract or contingency during the planning process exposes potential problems with the contract or contingency. It also enhances a common understanding of how execution should flow.

CLEAR COMMUNICATION

YOU MAY CAREFULLY DEVISE a truly formidable plan that sets your team up for success, but without clear communication, it is a complete waste. Fighter pilots use the brief as the flight lead's opportunity to ensure that team members are on board with exactly how we plan to execute the mission. The plan must be clearly communicated and understood to be effective. Fighter pilots use these briefs to "chair fly" their team through the mission. When I brief, my goal is for my wingmen to know exactly what is expected of them at all times during the mission. The more they know about the mission, the better. Clear communication is critical for mission success. To optimize our limited time, usually 60 minutes, fighter pilots have a repeatable briefing structure to make it easier to follow and provide maximum clarity, and it always starts the same way.

"30 seconds to 0600 Local...10 seconds...5...3, 2, 1, hack, the time is 0600 Local." Every flight brief starts with a time "hack." Traditionally, these time-hacks are meant to get us all to step, start our engines, taxi, and takeoff at exact times, so everyone always knows where we will be. However, with GPS updated watches and precise clocks in our jets, this purpose is outdated. The time hack serves a different purpose today. It is a way of establishing an expectation that the briefing will start exactly on time, and we will be disciplined and precise in all we do. There is no ambiguity about when the brief will start, and it sets the tone for the rest of the mission. It is not necessary or expected to show up to the briefing room 10 minutes early. You would be sitting there awkwardly looking at each other until the "hack." There is something more productive you can do with that time.

That is what it comes down to: valuing everyone's time. If I show up on time but sit around and wait for the briefing that starts 5 minutes late, then my time has been wasted. It is disrespectful to start late because it wastes the time of those who were ready for an on-time start. There is also no excuse to be late. The door closes at brief time—at the "hack." It is always precisely on time. Being late to a brief is a major breach of etiquette. If a fighter pilot were to show up late, they might not fly. It is that serious. It shows a lack of discipline, and again, a lack of respect for the time of others. Of course, there are extenuating circumstances, but the norm and the expectation is set. Being punctual shows respect.

It is a practice I think should extend beyond fighter pilot briefs. Have you ever had an appointment where you had to wait 10, 20, or even 30 minutes past your appointment time? Did it make you feel more appreciated, important, or valued? If you can help it, do not make people wait on you, whether that be your teammates or your clients.

Imagine a company that respects its clients' time. When they tell you that you will have a phone call appointment at 11:00 local, the phone rings at exactly 11:00. The client does not have to make him or herself available at 10:55 or wait until 11:05 for the phone to ring. That would waste their time. You have the opportunity to demonstrate that you value and appreciate your clients simply by respecting their time.

The time "hack" is followed immediately by a "welcome, today's mission objectives are…" The briefing starts with the end. What is our goal for this mission? Before discussing what we plan to do, we begin by stating what we aim to accomplish. Have you ever been in a meeting or briefing where you spent half the time trying to figure out what it was supposed to be about? Perhaps, you never figured it out at all. Did you ever leave a meeting where a lot of things were discussed, and even a lot of good points were brought up, but when you boil it down, nothing was accomplished? If you start every briefing, every meeting with the desired end result, it will help frame the rest of the time and keep everyone focused on the objectives.

ADMIN BRIEF: THE PATH TO EXECUTION

For every mission, a portion of the brief is dedicated to admin. This part of the brief is required for flight safety. It includes all the "goings and comings." Everything from when we leave the briefing room to when the "fight's on" happens for the tactical training, and then everything after the "knock it off" until we are back in the debrief room. Deconfliction and safety are paramount. The entire purpose is to get us all safely to and from the "fight airspace" and reinforce contracts for the fight that are necessary to operate safely. Although clean admin is incredibly important, fighter pilots do not like to talk about admin. Admin phases of flight often kill fighter pilots, but we would much rather spend our time talking about tactics and execution. To minimize the time that we need to talk about admin, and in turn, maximize our tactical briefing time, administrative standards are created.

Leadership in every squadron standardizes as much admin-related protocol as possible and publishes them so that these standards do not have to be briefed. Everyone in the squadron is responsible for knowing these standards cold. They include how we check in on the radio, what frequencies require a check-in, what time we will brief, step, and taxi, and how the radio calls should sound. They direct the default type of takeoff and approach to landing that will be flown and what formation we will fly to and from the airspace. Nearly everything in the administrative phase has a "standard." This gives the flight lead the ability to say in the brief, "Start, taxi, takeoff will all be standard," with no need to explain any further. This saves precious time. The standards provide an expectation. Everyone knows how things are supposed to operate. Standards are a baseline, but there are sometimes reasons to deviate from the standards. Knowing when to deviate is key, and I will talk more about deviating from standards later in this chapter when discussing tactical execution standards.

Although much of the admin brief can be briefed as "standard," there are a number of required items that must be briefed for every flight. These are essential safety items that cannot be briefed as standard, such as the "Training Rules (TRs)." TRs are the training limitations that have been developed over time and are commonly said to be "written in blood." Accidents may happen when these rules are violated. They are a big deal.

An example would be that aircraft must be "inside their block by 10 nautical miles without situational awareness (SA) on all players." The admin brief will establish altitude blocks for both friendly and adversary aircraft that keep us deconflicted as aircraft merge. If you know you are outside of ten nautical miles from the adversary, you are free to transit blocks and even fly inside of their block. However, once the "10 miles check blocks call" is made, all aircraft must get inside of their altitude blocks unless they have SA on where the other aircraft inside of ten miles are located. This keeps aircraft from running into each other. It is a vital contract that must be briefed every single sortie where air-to-air intercepts are occurring. Violations of these training rules are a big deal, and if there are any, they are always addressed in the debrief. Although standard, they must be briefed to bring them back to the forefront of everyone's mind because they are of supreme importance. It is vital to know what you can make "standard practice" for your team to set expectations and save time. It is also important to know what "standards" must be reiterated on a regular basis because they are just that important to your mission.

In the office, there may be established guidelines for fridge operations. Maybe there is a standard that you never leave your lunch overnight or that you mark your meal before placing it in the fridge. The tendency is for people to follow those guidelines for a few days, weeks, or in an exceptionally compliant office, maybe months. However, the more time that passes, the more likely people are to let those standards slip, and before you know it, there is a rotting bag of month-old egg salad stuffed in the deep recesses of the fridge. Drifting away from established standards is normal and calls for constant reminders. Fridge operations are probably not critical to your mission, but they demonstrate the necessity to constantly remind people of what they should know anyway. With limited opportunity and time for communication, it is important to identify and reiterate the most important standards to minimize drift while leaving more time to focus on new considerations.

TACTICAL ADMIN BRIEF: THE SITUATION UPDATE

The tactical admin brief follows the admin brief and is meant to codify the tactical situation in everyone's mind. It starts with the tactical objectives to focus the team on the most important things it needs to accomplish to achieve the mission objectives. Then, they narrow the focus to achievable bite-size objectives that all work together to achieve mission success. The team leader will also brief the acceptable level of risk (ALR) and explain what that will mean for the team during the distinct phases throughout the briefing.

Next is usually when Intel will brief the mission overview to include the political and military situation discussed in the last chapter. As they brief individual teams, they will focus on specific capabilities of the threats as they relate to that team. What is most urgent and important that this team needs to know about the threat to be effective? They will also brief any intelligence updates that have occurred since planning. These updates could include updated locations for high-value targets or surface threats that have moved or new enemy tactics observed in recent missions. Information is power when it is focused on what is important for the situation. Intelligence has a **LOT** of information. The key is knowing what information is important to what people. What information does this team need to succeed on this mission? This is what needs to be briefed. It is the responsibility of team leaders to make sure they are getting the key intelligence they need for their team.

The tactical "housekeeping" is completed by turning the attention back on the team to what the team's capabilities will be for this mission and what Rules of Engagement (ROE) govern our operations. The munitions loadout is one of the primary considerations. It is essential to know who is carrying what on your team. Knowing what everyone on your team brings to the fight allows real-time execution decisions. In execution, I want to know exactly who I can utilize to drop another bomb or shoot an untargeted contact. This will be dynamic based on expenditures, but understanding where the missiles and bombs are on your team and how they are expected to be employed will enable faster decision-making during execution.

The Rules of Engagement (ROE) dictate under what conditions these munitions are allowed to be employed. ROE is specified for both Air-to-Air and Air-to-Ground. The Air-to-Air ROE include Lack of Friendly (LOF) indications, Positive Enemy Indications (PEI), Hostile Act, or Hostile Intent. There is a commonly used criterion for Air-to-Air ROE, but it will change slightly based on the mission. For example, on one mission you may be able to satisfy PEI by observing an aircraft takeoff from an enemy airfield. However, on another mission, this may not satisfy PEI if the airfield is dual use with commercial airliners occasionally launching from the same airfield. In this case, we must rely on other means for achieving PEI. ROE is mission dependent and further varies with the strategic environment.

Air-to-Ground ROE tends to vary much more widely based on the target and the political and military situation. ROE in a large-scale conflict may be very easy to satisfy, and weapons release authority will almost certainly reside with the flight lead. However, even in these large-scale conflicts, attacking certain targets may have differing requirements and approval authorities. In more limited wars, ROE is usually much more restrictive. When I was flying in Iraq and Syria, most of the bombs I dropped required a general's approval. Additionally, we were incredibly careful to execute thorough collateral damage scans with our targeting pods. I am grateful that the appetite for civilian casualties was extremely low, and I had confidence in every bomb I dropped. Every mission is different, and the key is making sure your team has crystal clear guidance on their boundaries. Left and right boundaries take away ambiguity and set an expectation for execution.

EXECUTION BRIEF: "CHAIR FLY"

The execution brief is the meat and potatoes of the briefing and where fighter pilots want to spend most of their time. Fighter pilots do not become fighter pilots to learn how to fly from point A to point B. That is of little to no interest to us. We want to execute tactics. That is our highest and best purpose. Not doing paperwork, not doing endless additional duties, but executing fighter tactics in a fighter aircraft.

Fighter jets were not designed to transport cargo or people. These roles and the excellent pilots and crews that perform them are vitally important, but fighter jets serve a different purpose. Fighter jets are designed to do battle. That is their highest and best purpose. This is where we need to spend the bulk of our allotted briefing time. It is where our time and energy are best spent. The same is true for any person. You have a highest and best purpose that is the best use of your time and energy. I am not saying you will not have to do other, more administrative duties or that you should avoid them altogether. They are necessary in many cases, but you should make every effort to maximize the time you spend on your highest and best purpose. This requires looking for creative ways to standardize, delegate, or otherwise minimize the time you spend on lesser tasks to only what is necessary. Maximize your time on the best use of your time. For fighter pilot's "chair flying" execution is of supreme importance to mission success. During this rehearsal, the briefing will focus on three primary items: the **expectation** of how the mission will go, the **contracts** that are most important to the team and its success, and the **contingency** game plans in case things do not go as expected.

To be most impactful, execution briefs need to tell a story. The story explains the chronological progression of what will happen and how we are going to execute as a team during the mission. The story serves as a dress rehearsal for the mission. It also is a way of molding the minds of your team members to form a more cohesive unit. The job of the briefer is to make execution easier for the rest of the team. Additionally, the briefing flight lead must make sure his backup flight lead (#3 in a 4-ship) is up to speed on the plan so that if the flight lead is not able to make it to the battle for any reason, the mission can still proceed. Setting the team up for success is all about clear communication of a simple plan with well-defined roles for each team member throughout the mission. Time is a precious commodity for briefings, and it is impossible to cover every detail of the mission. To have time to highlight the most important parts of a mission, the flight lead must utilize published execution standards to optimize their time.

Standards set an expectation, but they are not law. They are usually the 90 percent solution. They give you a prescription for different common situations, but they are not blanket medicine. Standards are similar to protocol in medicine. Protocol gives you a baseline, a starting point for care. They explain how to treat a condition under normal circumstances. Treatment standards help doctors provide more consistent care and keep doctors in a hospital on the same page. They streamline care and expectation. I would contend that most of the time they are perfectly adequate. However, they are not always the best solution in different circumstances. Not all patients are the same, so there must be critical thinking to determine if the usual protocol provides the best care for an individual patient. If medicine were as easy as following protocol, it would not take years of intensive medical training and residency to become a doctor. A monkey or computer program can be taught to follow protocol for a whole lot cheaper than a doctor. Doctors have incredible expertise that allows them to follow standards when it makes sense but, more importantly, deviate when necessary to provide better care. If you cannot explain your standards and why they make sense for a given circumstance, you will not know when to deviate.

Similarly, critical thinking team members will not be convinced that you know how to navigate them as a leader. I fear our culture is moving further and further away from critical thinking to blind trust in systems and the expertise of professionals who follow "protocol." I have no problem with protocol and standards of care. They are important and useful, but dutiful adherence to protocol or standards without critical thought is a recipe for disaster. The key is knowing the standards and why they are the standards. That will empower you to know when to deviate from standards. To deviate, you must have a good reason, but if you never deviate, you probably either do not know what you are doing or have not been empowered to make decisions. Standards should be treated as guidelines, not law.

Fighter pilots break down every part of the mission to formation, sensors, energy, and communication. At each phase, I want my team to know exactly where I want them to be, what I want them to be doing, how I want them to get there, and what I want to hear them communicate. Some of this will be in accordance with our tactical standards. If it is, all I need to say is that this portion will be "standard." If it is a building block sortie where we are practicing the basics, I may elaborate and instruct on techniques to do this most efficiently. However, if it is a complex mission, I will brief it as standard unless I need to deviate for some tactical reason. This saves time. When my flight knows exactly where I expect them to be at all times throughout the mission, they can focus on what they are doing. I do not want them wondering, "what should I do now?" or "what does One want me to do?" I want focused aviators that know exactly what is expected of them and when. I want them to know the goals and exactly how we plan to achieve them every step of the way.

The brief is about telling the story. The story of how I expect everything to go. Where I expect everyone to be. What I want everyone to do. I will emphasize anything that will not be in accordance with our execution standards to make sure everyone is on the same page. I will also emphasize execution standards that will be especially important for that particular mission's success. Although my team already knows to execute those standards, they are vital enough that I will restate them in the brief to make sure it is fresh.

Know what you can call standard. Know when you need to deviate from the standards and communicate that clearly. Know when you need to emphasize a standard so it is fresh for execution.

As briefs flow through each phase, special attention needs to be paid to the contracts established in that phase. The contracts that are fleshed out in the planning phase are useless if the team does not understand them. For example, the Strike Team Lead could develop a contract with the ISR team lead to have an asset pass coordinates directly to a particular fighter formation when the location of a certain target is known. This may be a well-defined and appropriate contract that expedites the kill-chain and helps achieve mission success. Both leads may understand and know the contract well. However, if the system operator on board that asset does not understand that contract, he may send the information to the wrong formation or in an unusable format. Worst case, the information is not sent to anyone at all. The mission fails because the contract was not understood by all key players.

Unfortunately, this happens all the time. There is a wonderful plan that is easily executable, but it is not understood. It must be understood. Therefore, there must be special emphasis on key contracts in the brief. No one can leave that briefing room without a clear understanding of the contract. A great plan is not enough.

When briefing the contracts, or anything for that matter, it is important to make meaningful eye contact with the key players. Non-verbal feedback like North and South head nods can give you the warm-fuzzy that you are being understood. Conversely, when you get the confused looks from your audience, you know to take extra time to clarify the contract. "Rock-drilling" contracts are usually done during the planning portion of a mission, but when briefs are being done at the team or flight level, it is helpful to do this exercise on a much smaller scale. It is every team lead's responsibility to make sure everyone on their team is up to speed on all the contracts that they are responsible for or may affect their execution.

Contingencies are covered at the end of each phase of the brief to address the "what ifs" for that phase. It is important to note that these contingencies typically come after the expected flow and contracts are covered. If you continuously interrupt your story with what-ifs, it will quickly become disjointed and hard to follow. Conversely, if you do not clearly communicate your contingency game plan to your team, you are setting yourself up for failure when you inevitably experience a problem. There is a balance here. Some briefers like to hold contingencies until the very end of the entire brief, so their flow is not interrupted at all. This technique does have the advantage of keeping your story clear and uninterrupted. However, you do not get the benefit of showing your team how contingencies will impact your game plan as clearly when you do not include any in the bulk of the brief. People may have a tough time applying your contingency contracts in this case.

I have found the most effective way to communicate contingencies is at the end of each phase. "Ok, that's how we expect things to happen, but let's talk about some contingencies." Everyone then knows the ideal situation we expect; now, what if things do not work out as we are hoping. What if we are a three-ship instead of a four-ship. What changes? These contingencies were all developed during the planning portion, but again, unless they are understood, they are useless. Briefing these contingencies once again sets the expectation for the team.

Question marks in your team members' brains spell disaster in combat. Setting expectations help limit the number of question marks your team will have. "If, then" statements set these expectations. Briefings are limited, and you can never identify all of the "if, thens" for any mission. The planning period is the time to identify as many "ifs" as possible so you can develop the "thens." You will never have time to brief all of the possible outcomes for your mission, and your team will never have the bandwidth to retain all of the "if, then" statements you come up with in planning. You must prioritize the most important and most-likely contingencies, so they are fresh and executable for your team.

Have you ever experienced the anxiety that comes from not knowing what your boss wants from you? Have you ever started down a task hoping you are satisfying your boss, but worried it might all be a waste of time? It is frustrating. These are the situations you want to avoid like the plague as a leader. You never want question marks in your team's heads because it produces inefficiencies, wasted effort, and unhappy workers. Lack of guidance or incomplete guidance can create a work culture of uncertainty that allows for drifting away from your objectives. When the unexpected comes, you must be very clear and directive with your team. Do not assume your team knows what you want as a leader. Good leaders will constantly guide their team toward meeting their objectives even when they feel they are being repetitive.

The brief is how fighter pilots ensure the entire team understands the plan and is prepared for execution. Your plan may be the greatest, most technically sound game plan that, if executed perfectly, can never fail. However, if you fail to clearly communicate it to your team, it will never succeed. Mission success depends on your ability to develop an executable plan and then clearly communicate it to your team, so everyone knows their role in achieving the mission objectives. Maximize time and emphasize the most critical items necessary for mission success. Creating standards can streamline execution and limit time spent on less vital considerations.

Make sure your team knows the assumptions, purpose, and intent for these standards so they can deviate when it makes sense. When possible, communicate the plan in a chronological manner in bite-size "phases." Make sure all team members always know their roles and responsibilities throughout execution. Finally, prepare your team for contingencies by highlighting the most likely and most dangerous contingencies in each phase, so your team is ready if they occur. If you start with a simple, executable plan and then communicate that plan clearly, so all team members know their roles and responsibilities at all times, you will significantly increase your team's performance in execution.

SUMMARY FOR APPLICATION

1. **Start meetings on time and manage time through the admin and tac admin portions of your briefs to maximize time for execution.** Starting exactly on time sets the tone that precision matters and execution will be crisp. Maximize time for the execution brief by creating standards and only highlighting the critical administrative items necessary to pave the way for execution. The Tac Admin brief wraps up the necessary housekeeping by painting the picture of the problem, evaluating the available assets, and determining the acceptable amount of risk to achieve the briefed objectives.

2. **During the execution brief, you should "chair fly" for your team:** Walk through execution by logically focusing on the most important execution considerations. Having execution standards and using them frees up time to brief mission-specific items in more detail. However, it is vital to know the assumptions for your standards so you can deviate when necessary. The execution brief should tell the story of the roles and responsibilities of team members throughout execution.

3. **Focus on contracts and contingencies:** Contracts must be emphasized and clearly understood to be effective, so everyone understands their responsibilities. Brief the most likely and most dangerous contingencies, so the team is not caught off guard when they occur in execution. Make sure your team understands and does not have any questions by reading body language and asking questions.

FLEXIBLE EXECUTION

BEFORE I JOINED THE Air Force, I had built an image of fighter pilots and what flying fighters must be like from movies like "Top Gun." I do not think I am alone in that. When people find out I am a fighter pilot, they often say things like, "Wow, that must be exhilarating," or ask me, "Do you just love it?" I think people often think of it as an unmatched thrill ride. It certainly can be! I have had the privilege of flying a number of "incentive" and "familiarization" sorties in the F-15E, where I had a non-flyer in the backseat. I have flown maintainers, aircrew flight equipment, flight doctors, and intelligence troops as part of programs to reward outstanding performance or bring a new perspective and appreciation for what we do and how they can better support the mission. These missions are more like what people normally think.

I flew one incentive ride for a maintainer when my squadron was at Exercise Northern Edge in Alaska. Incentive flights are often dedicated to the individual rewarded with the flight with no real tactical purpose. However, on this sortie, we were tasked with providing "red air" for a Defensive Counter Air mission. Our goal was to simulate enemy aircraft trying to get past "blue" forces to bomb a target. This was probably the most fun I ever had on a flight.

We took off from Eielson Air Force Base and flew over Denali National Park on our way to our fight airspace. The view was incredible. Glaciers and towering mountains covered in snow give you a sense of awe and wonder and the greatness of our Creator. Once we got there, we "topped-off" our fuel tanks by aerial refueling from a KC-135 before starting the fight. Very, very few incentive flyers ever get to experience this from the fighter side of the exchange. The precision and coordination to maneuver an aircraft into a very small window just behind a 737-body aircraft and maintain a stable platform for over 10 minutes take loads of focus and practice. The refueling would mean we had approximately 32 thousand pounds of gas, much more than needed for the tactical mission. We executed a couple of low-altitude ingresses trying to make our way to the target. We got close a couple of times, but the blue forces were able to shoot us down before we were able to release our payload.

Once the flight was "knocked off," the real fun began. We had about 20 minutes of extra gas to really "incentivize" my back-seater before we hit "bingo." The mountains in Alaska are incredibly beautiful, and the terrain makes for the best low flying in the world. As an F-15E Strike Eagle pilot, I had flown countless low-fly missions. We love to fly low and fast, and we do it often. Nothing I had done previously could compare.

Flying nearly 600 MPH through mountain valleys with massive snow-covered peaks on either side is an experience that is hard to describe. I would command a 30-degree nose-high climb in afterburner to clear a ridge, then roll inverted to 120 degrees of bank. Then, staring up the top of the canopy to watch the ridge peak clear below us, I would dive aggressively back towards the ground into the valley on the other side of the ridge. Moments like that are pure joy. The awe, the wonder, the freedom, and the power of the nearly 60,000lbs of thrust in cold air is intoxicating. Lighting the afterburners at low altitude throws you back in your seat and dilates your pupils. It was the best flying I had ever experienced, and my incentive flyer got to share it with me.

Most incentive flyers struggle with the G-forces and airsickness. Most of the time, they are begging for some straight and level flight to catch their breath and ease their stomachs within minutes of take-off. These flights rarely last more than an hour, and many times the incentive flyers are begging to land early. Not this time. This time, my incentive flyer was in for a three-hour sortie that was the adventure of a lifetime. The response when we land is almost always the same. Pale white skin, full puke bags, and an appreciation for being safely and securely back on solid ground. They are exhausted and ready for a nap. "Wow, I can't believe you guys do that every day. That's really hard!" The truth is these are always the simplest and easiest flights we do. Relatively, they are not hard, either physically or mentally, for the pilots. Fighter pilot execution is about so much more than just flying an aircraft and handling the physical toll of fighter maneuvering.

Fighter pilots very rarely have the opportunity to "enjoy" the flying the way we do on incentive flights. The training we accomplish on a day-to-day basis is meant to make us lethal aviators. It is hard, and not just physically. It is extremely mentally taxing. Instead of simply enjoying the flying, your enjoyment becomes more about the challenge and the satisfaction you get from accomplishing something very difficult. When the tactical situation erupts and starts to become overwhelming, it is exciting. After a mission like this, it is common for fighter pilots to exchange comments like "That was insane!" with big smiles on their faces. When everything goes exactly as planned, it is almost disappointing. When things are easy, it is disappointing, boring. If things are easy in training, that means you did not design a hard enough training scenario to really challenge yourself and your team. Fighter pilots love the challenge of execution. To be effective in execution, you need a good plan that is communicated clearly in the brief, then implement it knowing the environment of aerial combat is fast-paced, dynamic, and unforgiving. Your plan should accommodate flexibility in execution.

FLEXIBILITY

"Flexibility is the key to airpower."
—GENERAL GIULIO DOUHET

General Douhet was an Italian general whose early and groundbreaking theories on the importance of air power and strategic bombing helped shape the history of military aviation. General Douhet's quote is one of the best-known adages in the USAF. Everyone knows it. It is so commonplace that it is used sarcastically or facetiously more often than seriously. Airmen often quote Douhet in jest when it is clear a plan or process is deeply flawed and will require massive deviations from the "plan." Furthermore, sometimes the rigid inflexibility of the Air Force bureaucracy is incredibly frustrating, highlighting the irony of an institution that claims to recognize flexibility as the key to airpower. This inflexible bureaucracy is one of our nation's greatest vulnerabilities. For example, we have a broken acquisitions process that directly threatens our ability as a fighting force to stay one step ahead of our enemies. This process desperately needs more flexibility, and I am hopeful we are moving in that direction. Fighter pilots embrace the need to be flexible. It is the most exhilarating and treasured part of execution.

Plans rarely, if ever, are executed with no need for real-time adaptation. We talked extensively about contingency planning for different scenarios where we identify a vulnerability. This, once again, helps us think through solutions before we are faced with them during execution. It is impossible, though, to identify every single possible scenario and the specific circumstances surrounding that scenario. Maybe the adversary does something unexpected. Now I must make a quick decision with all the macro considerations we had during planning, but none of the time. This need for decisiveness applies not only to fighter pilots, but to leaders in all areas of expertise. Not making a decision is a decision in itself. Indecision is almost always the wrong decision. There are times when it works out that not changing anything was the right decision, but that must be a conscious choice. Otherwise, you are relying on luck to win.

Furthermore, execution of the designed game plan is rarely flawless, and execution failures can create new, unexpected challenges. For instance, my air-to-air game plan may rely on my number Four being able to execute targeting responsibilities on a two-ship of J-11B Chinese Flankers taking off from an enemy airfield. He is responsible for monitoring and engaging aircraft taking off from that airfield. In the mighty F-35, this should be a very executable game plan. However, what if his radar fails at the exact time he is about to take shots, and he is unable to employ? This would be an impossible scenario to dream up in the planning process. If we tried to think of every little nit-noid contingency, we would never take off. However, the plan would influence my decision-making in real-time.

When I hear, "Panther 04 unable shots, radar bent," I must think quickly. The situation is unique to this specific moment, but there is a macro level of understanding of battlefield awareness and possible solutions based on planning, training, knowledge, and experience. I must rapidly canvass my options and choose the best one in a timely manner. Otherwise, if we fail to target these J-11Bs soon, we could put the entire strike package at risk. Time is the enemy. The longer I wait, the more complex the solution becomes. The plan may inform me that the "Eagle" flight has missiles available. Based on the plan and my real-time sensor awareness of where Eagle is located, I can confidently direct "Eagle 01 target two-ship Bullseye 258-58, hostile flanker."

Decisiveness is an essential quality for any leader. Being flexible and decisive is easier when you have confidence from understanding the plan and its vulnerabilities, and you have the authority to make decisions.

RISK MANAGEMENT AND DECISION MAKING

Risk management and decision making are gradable items on every training flight, starting from pilot training through the instructor course. It is vital. When I am sitting in my F-35 cockpit, it is just me. I am the mayor of cockpit city. I must be able to make decisions weighing the risks and alternatives, all while flying faster than the speed of sound. I am responsible for decisions about who lives and who dies. I must decide if going inside a threat ring is warranted or if our package has enough resources and capabilities to reattack a target. When things break down, I must continuously assess the risk and decide if I meet the overall mission risk. Fighter pilots are given extraordinary responsibility. This responsibility grows with experience and qualifications, but even the basic "wingman" is entrusted with incredible power and responsibility.

At 25 years old, I completed all my training to become a mission-qualified wingman in the F-15E, and I was handed the "keys" to a 50-million-dollar war machine. Imagine that…10 years prior, I was not even allowed to operate a car, and now this. I was tasked with defending our nation against its enemies. The tip of the spear.

A short two years later, I would be leading combat sorties over the skies of Iraq and Syria as a flight lead. The decisions I was empowered to make would have life and death consequences. Not only that, but they could also have worldwide consequences, especially when flying in close proximity to Russian aircraft over foreign airspace. Just two years after that, I would finish my upgrade to become an Instructor Pilot in the F-15E. At just 29 years old, I was now responsible for molding the next generation of fighter pilots, teaching them how to manage risk and make smart decisions with conviction. The fighter pilot community demands progression and growth. It also enables that growth by empowering young fighter pilots to make decisions and make them better, faster. Risk is necessary for growth, so how do you manage it wisely?

You may be familiar with common risk management techniques like Risk Avoidance, Risk Mitigation, Risk Acceptance, and Risk Transfer. Risk transfer is not really an option for fighter pilots. In aerial combat, I think of risk management as a dance between avoidance, mitigation, and acceptance. The lines are constantly blurred, continually bouncing between the three to achieve the mission. The mission is never to avoid all risks. There is no way to avoid all risks. Even jumping in that fighter jet and starting the engines came with risk. The aircraft are incredibly high-performing war machines that are intentionally unstable and routinely pushed to their maximum capability. Risk is necessary to accomplish the mission, but we want to avoid unnecessary risks.

There are times when I can simply avoid a specific risk, and it has no adverse effect on my ability to achieve the mission. If there is a threat system that I can simply avoid on my way to my target, then that is an easy decision. If a threat system is a factor for my target attack, it may be necessary to destroy that threat before it becomes a factor to my team or me. This may be feasible within mission constraints, but if not, I may have to mitigate the risk to the max extent possible by limiting my vulnerability window. I want to spend the minimum time practical exposed to the threat while also utilizing my other tools to mitigate the threat, such as countermeasures or electronic attacks. You can almost always reduce risks that you are forced to accept. There is likely something you can do to limit the time you are exposed to a risk or lessen the risk's probability of an adverse effect. When fighter pilots accept risk, we are always looking for ways to smartly mitigate that risk. In all cases, we strive to abide by the maximum acceptable level of risk that was "bought" for the mission. If it appears that the maximum amount of risk will be exceeded, we reassess our game plan. Success is accomplishing the mission objectives while not exceeding the acceptable level of risk, thereby incurring unacceptable losses.

For example, financial advisors are trained to assess the risk tolerance of an individual investor before making any recommendations. The client is the one that is "buying" the risk making it vital for the advisor to know exactly how much risk is allowed. Advisors usually rank this risk tolerance on a scale of one to ten, with ten being the riskiest. This is a common tool used to determine how much risk you are willing to "buy." If you are found to be a six, the decision is nearly always a portfolio with approximately sixty percent stocks and forty percent bonds. While that general asset allocation may be appropriate for some clients, it may not be optimal to fulfill the ultimate objectives of every client. If the client requires a return of five percent to meet their goals, but this portfolio is likely only to return four percent, then a conversation must take place to see if the client is willing to accept more variability in returns to achieve their goals. What is the larger risk: accepting greater variability in my returns or accepting a higher probability they will fail to achieve their objectives? It may ultimately be less risky to add more equities to their portfolio to increase the probability they meet their goal. Conversely, if they can achieve their goals with less risk, it may make sense to reduce their equity exposure even if they were willing to "buy" more to meet their goals. Most people do not consider that every action or inaction comes with risk. If I leave all my money in cash under the mattress, does that mean I am risk-free? Absolutely not! Inflation may erode the value of that cash over time, and you risk never acquiring the assets you need to achieve your financial goals.

Risk management is also complex because risk is not linear. If you think about risk on the margin, it makes decisions easier. If I accept one unit of additional risk, what does that buy me? If I fly one mile closer to this threat, what does that buy me? If I increase my equity exposure by one percent, what does that buy me? Is that marginal gain worth any additional exposure that will incur? In a highly functioning organization, the individual or team can "buy" marginal risk as they deem necessary, but never to exceed the overall risk "bought" by the leader/organization to achieve the mission objective.

One of the indicators of an effective leader is how well their team members make decisions. To empower team members to make sound decisions, a leader must give the team members confidence to make those decisions. This confidence is not gained through competence alone. Yes, the team member must understand the plan, the leader's intent, and have the expertise necessary to know he is right. However, there is another essential ingredient. Trust in the leader to back the decisions that were made in good faith. How the leader responds to a mistake in judgment by a team member will either build or destroy this trust. In the military, I have seen commanders who punished mistakes to "maintain good order and discipline." The result is always the same. It erodes trust in the leader and encourages followers to freeze or be distracted when they need to make decisions out of fear of how they will be judged by the commander.

There is a big difference between mistakes made in good faith and lapses in judgment where there is ill intent or negligence. Ill intent or negligence may warrant punishment. True mistakes require mentorship and guidance to grow and enable better decisions in the future. Making a habit of punishing mistakes will erode trust and make sound decision-making by team members significantly more challenging. The alternative is not to ignore the mistakes but to provide guidance, mentorship, and leadership to improve decisions through the growth of team members. This will empower your team to deal with the risk decisions that are inevitable.

There is risk associated with everything. Any action or inaction comes with risk. If you think you can avoid all risk, you are sorely mistaken. If you choose not to exercise, you risk all sorts of adverse health effects. If you choose to exercise, you risk injury from pulling a muscle, getting a cramp, or even having a heart attack from over-exertion. The risks are not equal either in probability or severity. Every medication has side effects that pose a risk to your health. Likewise, not taking the medication carries its own risk. The point is everything has consequences. You must decide based on the probability and severity of the risk and whether it is worth accepting. You must accept some level of risk to achieve your objective, no matter what it is. In fact, sometimes inaction is riskier than action.

CAPITALIZING ON OPPORTUNITY WITH VIOLENCE

I consider myself to be an analytical person. I like to compare various system capabilities to exploit weaknesses in the adversary's defenses. I want to make sure I set myself up for success. I would like to have the perfect geometry with the perfect assets to win without question. That is what good planning is all about. In war, as in life, it is about more than just pitting systems against systems. There are people involved. There is emotion, operator competency, confusion, deception, etc. You can exploit not only the system but also the person or team. In a well-planned and coordinated attack, it is usually advantageous to execute swiftly and violently to overwhelm enemy defenses by massing our firepower.

When we execute a well-coordinated attack with A/A Escort, SEAD, and Strike in perfect geometry, it is overwhelming for the enemy. It is violent and extremely effective. However, if during the initial strike some targets were missed, or there is a dynamic tasking that requires us to re-attack, things can break down. Ideally, we are able to get back into that perfect geometry to re-enter the threat area. However, that can take time. The longer it takes, the more time the enemy has to recover. Think about it like this. We just punched the enemy right in the nose. I do not want to wait for their eyes to stop watering to strike again. I want to keep the enemy blurry-eyed and on their heels. The longer I wait, the longer the enemy has to launch additional aircraft and get backup systems online. The longer I wait, the longer the enemy has to regain their courage and man the posts they had abandoned. I want them still licking their wounds when I strike again. Furthermore, the longer I wait, the less gas and missiles my package will likely have. Sometimes accepting less than optimal geometry is less risky than waiting for the perfect opportunity that may never arrive.

Risk management is complex and non-linear. It requires balance and constant consideration. This is true in life and business as well. The pace may not be as fast, but the concepts are the same. For example, in business, consider a company that has the opportunity to gain a first-mover advantage with a new product launch. Suppose that company waits until conditions are perfect or slows down marketing and sales to regroup after their initial push into the market. It will allow other companies to catch up and eliminate their advantage. Instead of waiting until conditions are perfect, they need to capitalize on their opportunity with marketing and sales to overwhelm would-be competition and solidify their positioning in the market.

On the other hand, if they move too quickly without having the necessary manufacturing and inventory on hand to meet demand, they may be faced with significant logistical issues. This could erode customer confidence when products are on backorder. Consider when it is prudent to execute swiftly and violently with conviction, and do not take too much time to regroup for the next strike.

MANAGING TASK SATURATION AND CHANNELIZED ATTENTION

I mentioned before that modern aerial combat is extremely dynamic and challenging. There is so much going on that it can be hard to manage. There is so much information to consume, and that information is constantly changing. You must make split-second decisions constantly. It is extremely mentally taxing. What do you do when things become overwhelming? What do you do when you just have too much to handle? It can be paralyzing for a lot of people. Fighter pilots do not have the luxury of paralysis. It is something we are constantly battling and becoming task-saturated is not uncommon. If the mission is challenging enough, it is almost a guarantee you will become task-saturated at some point. There is so much going on, but you must keep performing. You must keep making decisions and keep your situational awareness high. Becoming "sucked in" by one task is something we call channelized attention. Channelized attention is when you focus so much on accomplishing one of the many required tasks that you start to lose the big picture. You start failing to do other required tasks in a timely manner. This is a real danger not only in the cockpit, but also in many positions of leadership and responsibility in the civilian world. Dealing with task saturation and combatting channelized attention is a skill that is learned and takes practice. After all, we would rather "sweat in training than bleed in war."

I cannot count the number of times in training I have seen fighter pilots, including myself, get behind their Air-to-Air timeline and allow things to snowball to the point that they trespass inside of a threat zone and take a missile in the face. The reason is rarely that they just did not know the threat range or decided to ignore it for some reason. The explanation is almost always that they failed to recognize where they were on their timeline because they were distracted. They were so focused on trying to fight through some electronic attack with their radar, make a radio call, verify a kill, take a follow-on shot, or find an untargeted group. There is almost always a mis-prioritization of tasks that results from task saturation and/or channelized attention. If they would have recognized they were about to trespass a threat range, they would have made the correct decision to defend themselves. Instead, however, they unwittingly prioritized something less important. I have fallen victim to task saturation and channelized attention more times than I would like to admit.

Handling task saturation is difficult. You cannot simply will yourself into being able to handle more. The answer fighter pilots sometimes give in jest is to "be better, stronger, faster, and more awesome!" The truth is you cannot increase your capacity to handle more in the moment. It will be a process of growth over time, and the more you practice handling more tasks, the more you are able to handle next time. It is the same concept as a muscle. However, you are not helpless to manage task saturation. The best solution to task saturation is prevention.

The key to preventing task saturation is anticipation. When fighter pilots get task saturated, we call this "being behind the jet." When you are "behind the jet," you are no longer anticipating what comes next, but simply reacting. When you react, you lose your ability to control a situation and manage your tasks appropriately. To get "ahead of the jet," you must anticipate what is happening next. It takes fewer brain bytes to accomplish a task you know is about to happen when you anticipate it. That, in turn, frees up more brain bytes to think about what is happening next so you can push your awareness forward. The more you can get ahead of the jet, the easier things will become and the less likely you are to become task-saturated. Getting behind the jet is easy to do, but once you are behind, getting back ahead is quite difficult. Ideally, you stay "ahead of the jet" the whole time. After all, "An ounce of prevention is worth a pound of cure." However, there will inevitably come a time when you become task-saturated. When task saturation occurs, it is vital that you learn techniques to prevent task saturation from channelizing your attention and causing you to mis-prioritize tasks.

The "cross-check" is a vital tool that fighter pilots use to prevent spending too much time on any one task. Fighter pilots develop a rhythm for their "cross-check" that changes based on role, task, and phase of flight. For example, we train our wingmen to "cross-check" their Formation, Sensors, Energy, and Comm throughout a tactical intercept. A wingman may look outside to maintain visual with his flight lead and in the correct position, then look inside at his radar display to check for hostile aircraft, then to his radar warning scope to see if there are any threats targeting him, then to his heads up display to check airspeed, altitude, and attitude, then back outside to his flight lead. He does all this while absorbing radio calls and determining if making one is necessary. A common tendency for a wingman is to become "sucked in" to the radar scope and have his cross-check start to break down. Spending too much time staring at the radar screen to try to find a contact or interpret the symbology can lead to getting out of formation with his flight lead, failing to react to a threat, getting too slow, or even finding himself upside down inside of a cloud.

The cross-check is vitally important, and it takes practice. Many tasks become muscle memory over time, and the better you get in the jet, the less time you need on certain tasks. So keeping that cross-check prevents bad things from happening. It keeps you from focusing your attention on any one thing to the detriment of more important tasks that may arise. You may be spending upwards of 70 percent of your time on the radar, but you have quick checks of your other sensors at regular intervals. The cross-check is more than just keeping your ears open; it is an active effort to maintain situational awareness. Keep your cross-check alive, and you will be less likely to become overwhelmed by task saturation. However, even with courageous attempts at prevention, you may still find yourself task saturated with channelized attention. This is a dangerous position, and in that moment, it is crucial to know how to recover.

"I have no idea what's going on, and even simple tasks seem overwhelming because I can't keep up." Have you ever felt that way? Have you felt like you have been thrashing around but cannot seem to get anything done? I sure have. Recovering from task saturation and channelized attention takes deliberate steps. The first step is to recognize what is happening. It seems obvious afterward, but sometimes it is hard to recognize when you are in the midst of it. We have a saying about situational awareness that "you don't know you've lost it until you get it back." You may recognize you are overwhelmed, but you have not consciously thought, "wait, I'm task saturated, and I need to do something about it." After the fact, it is obvious, but amid the chaos, you are just trying to tread water. If you find yourself becoming overwhelmed, the best thing you can do is take a quick pause. For aviators, this is a very, very quick pause to recover and get the cross-check back on track. Recognizing task saturation and pausing to allow yourself to calmly assess the situation can help avoid channelized attention and prevent the situation from becoming worse.

Here are four helpful steps to overcome task saturation:

1. Acknowledge the situation. You must recognize your actions have become reactionary, and you are focusing too much time and attention on one task.

2. Re-establish your cross-check so you can see clearly and analyze what needs to be done.

3. Start prioritizing tasks and accomplishing them based on importance and what needs to happen next while maintaining your cross-check.

4. Start pushing your "situational awareness bubble" out and forward.

While you may need to be focused on what you need to do right now, you must start anticipating the next task you need to accomplish as quickly as possible. This will prevent you from executing the wrong task as you continue to simply react to the perceived most pressing need. It will also allow you to frame the tasks you need to perform in a logical progression towards your goal. If you are simply reacting to tasks, you are not controlling the course toward the desired outcome. Once you are back in front, you can again work to prevent task saturation from occurring in the future.

Effective execution can be learned by practicing key concepts that can be widely applied. Starting with a well-developed and clearly understood plan will help make implementation more likely to succeed so long as flexibility is maintained. Maintaining flexibility in execution enables risk management decisions to be fluid and made on the margin within overall mission constraints.

Empowering people who operate on the margin to make those incremental risk decisions is possible when your team is fully on-board with the plan and competent. This empowerment will make your team more effective and efficient at completing tasks and accomplishing your objectives. When execution is complex, it is easy to become task saturated and channelize your attention on some tasks at the cost of other, more important tasks. Preventing task saturation by anticipating the next step in the logical progression is key to effective execution. When task saturation does occur, it is important to recognize it, resume your cross-check to analyze the situation, prioritize accomplishing tasks based on the logical progression of what needs to happen to meet your objective, and finally, slowly move your focus away from the immediate task at hand and back to anticipating what happens next.

In the next chapter, we will further explore the process pilots use to combat task saturation and channelized attention during incredibly high-stress emergency situations.

SUMMARY FOR APPLICATION

1. **Flexibility is the key to airpower:** Even well-constructed plans are rarely executed flawlessly with no need for real-time adaptation. Being flexible and decisive is easier when you have confidence from understanding the plan and its vulnerabilities, and you have the authority to make decisions.

2. **Risk Management and Decision Making in Execution:** Risk is a natural part of any venture and is necessary for growth. Knowing how much risk is acceptable and who is allowed to "buy" risk is vital to efficient execution. The individual or team should be empowered by leadership to "buy" marginal risk as they deem necessary, but never to exceed the overall risk "bought" by the organization leader to achieve the mission objective. Consider that it can sometimes be less risky to be aggressive when the opportunity presents itself than wait until the "perfect" conditions.

3. **Managing Task Saturation and Channelized Attention in Execution:** Task saturation is common and difficult to prevent. Prevention takes constant anticipation of the next task to stay ahead. When you have fallen behind, it is easy to have your attention channelized. The key is recognizing it, re-establishing your "cross-check," then prioritizing tasks and accomplishing them based on importance and what comes next.

CRISIS MANAGEMENT

My four-ship of F-15Es is about to take off out of Seymour Johnson Air Force Base to execute a Defensive Counter Air training mission. I am leading the four-ship on one of my last sorties in my upgrade to become a four-ship flight lead. Our mission objective is to protect the coast for 30 minutes from aggressing aircraft. It was scheduled as a 4 vs. 6 with six total red air that would be "regenerating" each time they were killed to represent a total of up to fourteen enemy aircraft. This is my favorite mission set. It is all Air-to-Air, and it is fast and furious. We have a simulated loadout of six radar-guided AMRAAMs, two heat-seeking Sidewinder missiles, and 510 rounds in the 20MM Gatling gun. This is my favorite mission, so I do not mind the added stress that comes with an upgrade. My WSO in the backseat is also on his upgrade ride. I am giddy as we light the afterburners and barrel down the runway, lifting off with three fighters in trail at my command.

I am laser focused. It is hard to describe the level of focus fighter pilots have when executing their mission. Compartmentalization becomes an essential skill, and fighter pilots are experts at it. They must focus exclusively on the task at hand. While executing, I can think of nothing else. My focus is entirely on the mission. It is exhilarating being so focused and sharp.

The mission is intense, but the 30-minute period we were assigned to defend the coast concludes with no bandits getting past our defenses. Now, we are in "overtime." Bonus training above and beyond our stated objective. Why not? It is fantastic training, and we want to squeeze every ounce of training we can get out of our remaining jet fuel. I shoot a missile at an enemy fighter that is now halfway through our desired engagement zone and quickly exit once the radar-guided missile is "active" and no longer needs my data-link support. The missile's own radar has turned on, and it is guiding to the enemy without my assistance. My exit is aggressive. I roll to greater than 90 degrees of bank and slice my aircraft through the air to turn my jet as quickly as possible away from the threat. This will preserve the range between my jet and the enemy so I can turn around again and execute a re-attack before I would be vulnerable to the threat. I do a quick cross-check of my wingman, who is in a decent position, then back towards my sensors.

Halfway through the turn, I feel the jet starting an un-commanded roll to the right. This could be a known flight control anomaly in this jet, so I initially do not think much of it. However, when I roll level, it still wants to roll right. I immediately check my master caution light and control panel to see if I have any failures. Nothing. That is strange; maybe I fell out of trim. I try to trim the aircraft with no luck. I then quickly check my fuel quantities to see if I have developed an imbalance that may be causing some roll. Everything checks out. That is weird, maybe it is nothing. I am able to control it just fine at these speeds. As flight lead, I run our "cold ops" procedure while running away from the enemy to allow our missiles to impact and re-group. Based on the threats remaining alive, I direct the flight to turn around and shoot all their remaining missiles at the alive bandits before exiting to retire as a formation. In these turns, I feel the same thing, but again I am able to control it, and nothing appears to be wrong from all my indicators.

As we start our return to base (RTB), I reform the formation to "close" so we can check our aircraft visually for any panels that may have fallen off or hung flares that may be a hazard for the RTB. "This is so weird," I think to myself, still analyzing my flight control situation. As we slow to the 300 knots for the RTB, it is taking more and more lateral stick pressure just to keep the aircraft level. I am up to ½ stick deflection now. There are no failures on my flight controls, and trim does not seem to be making a difference. I have checked my fuels now several times.

That is when I hear Four say, "One, your left aileron is fully deflected."

"Now that makes sense," I think to myself, "but why don't I have any cockpit indications of a flight control malfunction?" I have never heard of this happening before. I have a failed aileron that is fully deflected. In many aircraft, this would be unrecoverable. It would cause a roll that you could not counter and would lead to a crash. In the F-15E, our horizontal stabilizers can help generate more rolling action and counteract the roll from the aileron. For now, it is sufficient to maintain controlled flight.

I then hear Four, who is the Squadron Commander and an experienced Instructor Pilot, continue over the radio, "One, I recommend we clear off Two with Three and work this." I agree and get a separate clearance for their two-ship and clear them to RTB separately.

As we continue our RTB, our next step will be to execute a "controllability check" over an unpopulated area. This is the only checklist that applies as there are no other indications. There is nothing I can do to fix it; I just need to figure out if I can still land. We will slow to lower our landing gear and flaps and see if we can slow enough to land while maintaining aircraft control. I decide that my limit is ⅔ stick deflection. So, I will slow to either normal landing speed or ⅔ stick deflection, whichever happens first. If I can slow enough to land, we should be good. As we set up for the check, my WSO and I tighten our harness straps just in case we go out of control and need to eject. For a moment, my mind wanders to my fiancé, but then I am quickly back in the moment. As I slow below the F-15E's max gear speed of 250 knots, I am getting closer and closer to my ⅔ limit.

"One is gear now," I call over the radio to let Four know. Wonderful, I regained a little extra control. I am back closer to ½ stick deflection. Now I can slow further.

We end up slowing to about 20 knots faster than on speed. I want a little extra control authority from the increased airflow over my flight controls because when we check the weather at the field, we learn there are stiff crosswinds. Nearly direct crosswinds from left to right at 25 knots gusting to 35. Of course, now I must fight the wind that will also want to roll my aircraft. We maneuver the jet for a straight-in approach from about 10 miles from the field with Four in "chase" to monitor my landing. As I shift my aimpoint, I intentionally execute a less aggressive "flare" to allow the jet to touchdown with extra energy and control authority. As the main landing gear touches down, I have an immediate sense of relief. I quickly but gently lower the nose gear to the ground to avoid aerodynamic braking with a flight control malfunction. I hold full left stick pressure through the landing roll to help counteract the crosswind and keep the jet level.

As we slow to taxi speed, I hear my WSO say, "Thank God, nice work."

"That was wild," I reply, and for the first time, we start chatting about how sketchy that situation was.

"How did the aileron fail like that with no indications? I thought if they failed, they were supposed to streamline, not go fully deflected." This was true; I had never heard of anything like this happening. It is still the only instance to my knowledge. Thank God, indeed.

Although one of the most memorable, this is just one of the many aircraft emergencies I have encountered in my fighter pilot career. All pilots go through extensive training in how to handle emergencies. During pilot training, it is a massive emphasis. Before we can train someone to fly and learn complex mission sets, they must be able to handle emergencies. You must be able to handle them beginning with the first time you strap in. On your very first flight, you could have an engine fire that, if you do not operate correctly, could result in you ejecting or worse. Even if you do handle it correctly, you may still have to eject, so you better be prepared to do that as well. Trainees learn the basics and must execute emergency procedures to standards in the simulator before ever strapping into the jet. It is in the pilot's best interest to be entirely competent in handling emergencies.

Post pilot training and throughout a pilot's career, there is a regular emphasis on emergency procedures (EPs). Every briefing for every flight will include an EP of the day. Usually, the youngest, most inexperienced wingman will stand up and brief 2-5 minutes on an EP from the checklist that could occur on any flight. Sometimes these are tailored for specific missions, but often it is random since you never know what that day will bring. There are also semi-annual EP tests, monthly EP simulator sorties, and regular check rides in the simulator for qualification. The emphasis is there because it is important. Crisis management is essential for flight safety, and the Air Force does it well.

THE STEPS

In pilot training, when quizzed on how to handle an emergency by an instructor, the response always begins with the mantra, "Sir, I will MAINTAIN AIRCRAFT CONTROL, ANALYZE THE SITUATION AND TAKE THE PROPER ACTION, AND LAND AS SOON AS CONDITIONS PERMIT." These steps are burned into the brains of all aspiring pilots to highlight the priorities. They seem obvious, but there is a reason for the mantra.

Priority number one is to **maintain aircraft control.** Before you can do anything else, you need to get the aircraft under control and maintain that control through a disciplined cross-check. We have a saying, "The jet isn't going to just explode." There are very few cases of spontaneous catastrophic failure. For almost all emergencies, it is prudent not to do anything too hastily. That is how mistakes happen. Everyone has been in a crisis at some point where someone starts pan-icking and trying to do too much too fast. This is what you want to avoid. You want to avoid panic and remain calm. The first step is just to maintain control of the situation. The tendency when something goes wrong is to devote all your attention to figuring out what is happening and what you need to do to fix it. Like moths to a flame, it is hard not to immediately focus on the problem. Figuring out what is going wrong is important, but it cannot come at the price of distracting you from your number one priority of staying in control.

For fighter pilots, maintaining aircraft control means knocking off whatever you were doing before, transitioning to straight and level flight, turning on the autopilot if you have it, and pointing the jet towards a suitable airfield if necessary. You want to eliminate as much task load as possible to deal with the emergency safely and effectively. If you try to do everything at once, your mind just cannot keep up. You end up doing things poorly and quickly become task-saturated. Maintaining aircraft control is not just a step; it is a priority throughout the emergency. A thorough cross-check keeps you from channelizing your attention and potentially putting yourself in a dangerous position. Remaining calm through a crisis will make the next step much easier.

Now that you have control, it is time to **analyze the situation**. What has happened, and what does it mean? What systems are offline? What failure indications do I have? What is the most important thing I need to handle first? What are my options? It is so easy to jump to conclusions. Easy to feel the urgency to act and start down the wrong path. Once you start down that path, it can be challenging to recognize it was the wrong path to begin with. You start to get so focused on fixing the situation that you fail to recognize you are not helping at all. Your vector is wrong. Correctly analyzing the situation is the precursor to taking the proper action. If you analyze it wrong, it is impossible to take the appropriate action. This is where the importance of calm becomes so apparent. You have to take a deep breath and think logically.

Logic is hard when you are panicked. So how do you stay calm when your life is potentially on the line? Practice and knowledge. Practice the procedures. Practice the steps. Practice the priorities. The structured approach to dealing with emergencies helps. The more you practice that structure, the easier it will be to remain calm. You may have heard military members say, "You just have to trust your training." I agree that trusting your training to take over in high-stakes situations is important. You want some actions to be automatic and correct without even having to think about it. However, as effective for building knowledge and habit patterns as training is, for fighter pilots, the process that the training has ingrained is even more important. Fighter pilots practice a structured approach to handling emergencies so many times that you always know where to start. Training is not what keeps you from panicking; it is the confidence that training builds that is the key to success in crisis. I have confidence that approaching any emergency with this process works. I may not know exactly what is going on right away, but I know how to handle the crisis.

When you are in a crisis, it is prudent to fix the problem as expeditiously as possible because some problems can lead to other problems. However, rushing could cause you to misdiagnose the problem and start down a rabbit trail. By choosing too quickly, you could channelize your attention on the wrong task and fail to recognize your error until you have made things worse. When crisis strikes, do not rush. It is a natural reaction. You feel a surge of adrenaline and a need to react. Your heart can start pumping a little faster, and you feel it. You feel the urgency. You feel the need to act right now. For aircrew, it is about survival and protecting national assets from further harm. It is easy to allow this to narrow your vision. Take a deep breath; the situation will not just explode immediately. In most cases, that is. In all cases, analyzing the situation properly enables you to **take the proper action.**

Checklists exist to help pilots **take the proper action.** When a pilot has completed analyzing the situation and come to a conclusion concerning the problem, he will then reference the appropriate checklist. Emergency procedure checklists are compiled in a book with tabs that enable quick reference in flight for pilots. These checklists contain step-by-step actions for the pilot to take. They also often contain Notes, Cautions, and Warnings that highlight critical information about that emergency. The importance of the information is commensurate with the category the information is held under.

Notes are generally important information for the pilots' situational awareness, but they are generally not an immediate safety concern. Cautions highlight information that could become a safety factor if not understood and heeded. Warnings are big. Warnings tell pilots that there is a major safety concern, and you want to read and heed. Pilots are diligent to study the intricacies of systems ahead of time and should be familiar with these Notes, Cautions, and Warnings well prior based on their studies because there is not always time to reference them all during flight. Some checklists may have a lot of information in the form of Notes, Cautions, and Warnings, and it is important to know which you need to spend extra attention on.

Checklist discipline is something that is emphasized early on in pilot training. You must follow the checklist, and you cannot let yourself get sidetracked. A radio call, an altitude or airspeed change, a new indication, there are so many things that can distract you and get you sidetracked. Now, that does not mean I will not interrupt a checklist to address a more pressing and important concern. If my jet catches on fire while I am working on a Generator Failure checklist, I am most certainly going to address the more pressing and serious threat to life and equipment, then circle back to the generator problem later. That is less common, though.

A common tendency is to not complete a checklist. You execute a step that appears to fix the situation, and there is a sense of relief. "Phew, good, ok, I guess it's time for the 'land as soon as practical' step." Wrong! The next checklist step you skipped may direct one last vital switch change that will protect your aircraft from further damage or complication. Do you ever find yourself interrupting a task to address some new problem and then forget where you left off or never get back to your task? You can spend an entire day not getting anything accomplished, just a lot of half-tasks. Prioritization is important, and perceived urgency can lead to mis-prioritization. Just because it is a new problem does not mean it needs to be addressed right now. Do a quick mental "triage" of the new problem. If it truly is urgent and important enough to interrupt your current task, note where you are in your current task and address the higher priority. Otherwise, finish what you are doing, and move on.

Some emergencies require immediate attention. There is no time to reference your Emergency Procedures Checklist, and you must know what to do by heart because time is of the essence. Different aircraft communities may call these critical procedures by different names. Some call them BOLD FACE. Pilots are required to memorize the steps by heart and are regularly tested on these procedures. They are routinely required to write out the procedure in all CAPS to demonstrate they know exactly what needs to be done. Failure to memorize and correctly write out the BOLD FACE flawlessly with no spelling errors would result in being grounded. You cannot fly if you do not get it exactly right. No room for slop. Other airframes simply call these critical action items. The emphasis on importance is the same. You must know it flat.

These emergencies are urgent and important, but they still need to be diagnosed correctly and the corrective steps taken with great care. Take a deep breath to make sure you are doing it right. Imagine you are flying the twin-engine F-15 in a training mission over the Gulf of Mexico. You are 50 miles offshore when you hear a loud bang; then quickly, you see one of your fire lights illuminate. You have experienced an engine malfunction that has started a fire. You know exactly what to do. This is one of your "critical action item" checklists where you do not need to reference your checklist. You have memorized the steps. You reduce the throttles to idle to see if the engine recovers and the fire goes out. It does not. You then press the fire button that has been illuminated. The next step is to pull the throttle cutoff lever up and retard the affected engine OFF. You quickly rush through the steps with your heart beating a mile a minute. After you bring the throttle off, you feel thrust decrease significantly. When you look at your engine panel, you realize your mistake. "I've just shut down the wrong engine." Now, both engines are rolling back, and you have just made a bad situation much worse. These types of mistakes have happened. You are in such a hurry, for good reason, that you make a bad situation worse. Know when to take the extra time. Your jet will not explode.

Everything is more complicated when you are airborne. If I can just land…Everything becomes so much simpler. Therefore, you are always thinking, "Ok, is it safe to land this jet, or is there something else I need to do." Generally speaking, landing solves most problems for pilots. An engine that is about to quit is a lot less threatening on the ground than airborne. If I am on short final to land and I get an engine fire, guess what, I am landing that airplane, and then I will deal with the fire. However, If I am 20 miles out to land and I get an engine fire, then I am still going to land that aircraft, but I may need to execute some immediate checklist steps to make sure things do not get worse, and the jet burns up before I can land.

I want to **land as soon as conditions permit.** Sometimes that is right now, immediately since I am already there and the emergency does not prohibit landing. Other times, significant troubleshooting and checklist management are necessary to prepare the jet for landing. Checklists will sometimes dictate how you manage the urgency of landing. If the checklist directs to "Land as soon as practical," it means something very different than "Land as soon as possible."

"Land as soon as practical" means do not delay unnecessarily, but it is unlikely that taking a little extra time will have an adverse effect. "Land as soon as possible" means to find the nearest suitable piece of concrete and land the jet. A dangerous condition that could cause loss of aircraft may persist. The concept remains the same. Land when able to mitigate the risk. Again, it all comes back to risk management. Is it a higher risk to rush the recovery and potentially make a mistake, or delay too long and allow the situation to become worse? Everything has a different urgency and a different risk profile. I would like to end the risk by landing as soon as I am able.

LEARNING FROM CRISIS

Every emergency is reported through a safety office to track trends and highlight problem aircraft or systems. This is an important process for the Air Force to address problem areas in a timely manner. However, more importantly for pilots is the informal sharing of information from other pilots. I can read a short summary of every squadron emergency written by the pilot within 24 hours of the event. If it is a more significant event, pilots will communicate their stories in a weekly pilot meeting to the entire squadron. Every emergency has lessons to be learned. It does not matter how many times you have seen an emergency in the simulator, there is always something more to be learned from an actual flight experience.

This briefing is always open and honest. There is no holding back. There is no desire or attempt to cover up mistakes. That is what it is all about. What happened to me, what I did about it, and what could I have done better so we can learn for next time? Flying fighters, although you may be solo in the jet, is a team effort. The individual is far less important than the team. That does not mean the individual does not have value or can be discarded or replaced. It means that you care so much about the success of the people around you that you do not care if you highlight a flaw or failure in your own execution.

These principles are true outside the cockpit as well. How you handle a crisis will be a test of your leadership. People value humility, and they will generally have more compassion than you expect when you are open and honest. This is especially true when you are open and honest to benefit them because you care about their success. The next chapter will explore this in much greater detail as we examine the way fighter pilots debrief.

SUMMARY FOR APPLICATION

1. **Maintain aircraft control:** The first step to any emergency is to get and maintain control of the situation before you start trying to

solve anything. Your jet will not explode spontaneously, so there is no need to panic. You want to simplify things to make the next step easier. Eliminate as much task load as possible so you can deal with the emergency safely and effectively.

2. **Analyze the situation and take the proper action:** When emergencies occur, it is natural to want to do something immediately. The feeling of urgency can be overwhelming even when it is not time-critical. Slow down to analyze the situation before taking the proper action. Have systems in place to help counter panic and take the extra time to get your vector right. Then, take the appropriate action one step at a time.

3. **Land as soon as conditions permit:** Look for opportunities to reduce risk during emergencies. For pilots, landing will often reduce risk to near zero. What actions can you take to reduce your immediate risk exposure?

VITAL DEBRIEF

FOR FIGHTER PILOTS, THE most important part of any training mission is the debrief. This is where the bulk of the learning happens, so fighter pilots take it very seriously. We want to make sure we understand exactly what happened: what went well, what did not go well, and how to improve for next time. This may be the most important thing that fighter pilots do, and it is largely absent from the civilian world of business leadership. I am not saying that a comprehensive debrief is always necessary for every little project you complete. However, if you do not have a habit and process to efficiently improve performance by learning from events, you are stunting your growth. This is one of the main reasons why I am writing this book. It would be very helpful if the civilian world of business and industry learned from the Air Force how to do a proper debriefing. Fighter pilots cannot afford to waste learning opportunities, and neither can you!

My observation is that most organizations only debrief when something goes very wrong, and they need an After-Action Report. This makes me think of the quote from the popular movie *Top Gun* when Air Boss Johnson is mad at Maverick and Goose for doing another high-speed pass of the tower, and he yells, "I want some butts!"

They want someone held accountable for the failure. What they mean by that is they want someone fired, demoted, or otherwise blamed for the failure. That is not what fighter pilots are trying to accomplish with their debriefs. Fighter pilots have a vastly different and better view of what it means to be accountable. Debriefs are not only for when things go very, very wrong. Debriefs are for learning. Often, the most learning comes from missions that fail, but there can still be a lot of learning from missions that seem to go off without a hitch. What did we do that worked well, and can it be repeated next time? However, as I have stated before, there is no such thing as a perfect sortie. Even if things seemed to go well, there is always something you can improve. However, you want to be careful not to waste your team's time, so it is best to follow a process proven to improve performance.

Additionally, at nearly $40,000 per F-35 flying hour, we just cannot waste the resources. That means that a simple 4-ship sortie flying for an hour and a half costs approximately $240,000. That is not even including the adversary training aid aircraft we need to train against. Some Large Force Exercise training sorties that I have flown in have featured over eighty aircraft. Imagine that price tag…This is not even the primary reason fighter pilots feel responsible to optimize every minute of flying time. We are charged with the defense of the United States and her interests. We need to be the best. Efficient and effective debriefs help us to be the best.

KNOW YOUR GOAL

There is a slight difference in the way debriefs are run, depending on the scope of the mission and the (DLOs) Desired Learning Objectives. What is the goal for your debrief? Every debrief needs to be tailored to meet its objectives. For example, most LFE (Large Force Exercise) debriefs are rightly focused on integration and scrutinizing the plan. When you have 100+ aircraft and over 300 people involved in the mission debrief, it would be a waste to spend your valuable debriefing time on the tactical execution of any specific aircraft. Plenty of mistakes happen in an LFE, but the ones you want to spend the bulk of your precious time on are the ones that could have been prevented by better planning. That does not mean individual fighter pilots will not be highlighted if their error leads to mission fail. It means that in an LFE, something else is on trial. You want to know the holes in your plan. You spent an entire day on mission planning and trying to integrate all these different capabilities into one congruent plan. Did it work? What did you not think of during the planning process that the entire team can take away for the next time they integrate? How can we make this entire team more synergistic for future missions? The emphasis is different in a smaller flight debrief where you can focus on individual execution within the flight to make the individuals better. The key is to know the goal of your debrief and tailor it accordingly.

PERSONAL ACCOUNTABILITY IS PARAMOUNT: OWN YOUR MISTAKES, HAVE THICK SKIN, AND NO QUIBBLING

Fighter pilots must have thick skin to swallow their pride and own their mistakes in the debrief. We have discussed the importance of accountability in previous chapters, but I cannot emphasize it enough. You MUST own your mistakes. Fighter pilots enter the debrief knowing they will be held accountable for their mistakes. There is an expectation that if you make a mistake, you will own that mistake in the debrief. No one likes to look bad in front of their peers. It hurts. You never want to be the reason for a mission fail.

However, there is a culture in the fighter pilot community that respects personal accountability. When someone owns their mistake, you appreciate it. You know you can trust that person. This culture of accountability must be introduced early and reinforced regularly to be effective. In general, people do not want to admit fault. For some reason, it is seen as an admission to incompetence. This is easily apparent in politics. Politicians never seem to want to own their mistakes. It is seen to be politically damaging since it admits a flaw that can be perceived as incompetence. This is true not just of politicians. A desire to conceal faults is rampant in society. We have become so sensitive that we interpret any criticism as an attack on our character or personal worth. This sensitive mental state is incredibly damaging and prevents progress, trust, and unit cohesion.

I have had the opportunity to fly with pilots from various countries over my career. There is a clear difference in competency between fighter pilots that is a direct result of this culture of accountability. In cultures that emphasize the need to "look good" and not insult another pilot by pointing out their errors, performance suffers. In cultures that embrace personal accountability, such as our own, fighter pilots quickly grow to perform at high levels. The results are clear. We may be using the same, or similar equipment, but the outcomes are vastly different. It's the software (fighter pilots) that makes a world of difference.

Accountability is vital, but do not confuse accountability with punishment or retribution. Debriefs are purposefully non-punitive. The purpose of the debrief is not to play the blame game but to find out what went wrong and why. That takes accountability. Being held accountable does not mean you are punished or that your career is in any way negatively impacted. It means that we acknowledge and own our errors, and we insist that our wingmen acknowledge and own their errors.

We need to learn and get better as a team. If you made an error that led to mission fail, you better believe you will be held accountable for that error. However, when you leave the debrief, that is it. Your mistakes do not follow you. They only follow you in the sense that they help you and your team do better next time. Everyone can learn from everyone else's mistakes. That is why no one is spared in the debrief, even the colonel or general. Too often, we equate accountability with punishment. Nothing could be further from the truth in a fighter pilot debrief. I can learn from the mistakes my wingman makes and vice versa. It is not about judgment; it is about learning and growth.

Fighter pilots have the advantage of having all their displays taped. You can see exactly what everyone did at every second of the flight. We have the "truth data." It is not easy to watch your tapes knowing you made a mistake that everyone else is about to see. This takes thick skin. No one is going to ignore your mistakes. It does not matter if you are a brand new Lieutenant or a General. Your mistakes are on display for all to see, and they will be highlighted. In some cases, there will be an excruciating amount of time dedicated to one mistake if that mistake caused mission fail. It can hurt. It is not fun, but you better believe you will learn from that experience and be committed to never making that mistake again.

There are reasons, and there are excuses. It is rare that someone just intentionally messed up. There is always a reason. However, it is a very thin line between reasons and excuses. People will routinely mistake their excuses for reasons. Excuses are disgusting and frowned upon in fighter pilot debriefs. As mentioned in Chapter 4, we call it "quibbling" when you start making excuses for what happened. If I were to claim in a debrief, "I didn't shoot on time because, Two, you distracted me by being out of position, and I was trying to tell you to get back into position, and I missed my cue to shoot." That is an excuse. That is a failure to own a mistake. It may be perfectly valid that number Two was out of position, and it distracted me, but I still made a mistake that I need to own.

Owning the mistake would sound something more like, "I messed up and failed to shoot on time. I allowed myself to become distracted by Two being out of position and mis-prioritized my tasks. I should have focused on shooting on timeline and then communicated for Two to get back into position." That is owning a mistake. There is a reason you made the mistake, and number Two should fix it for next time, but it is still your mistake. No one forced you to shoot off timeline. You simply allowed an external stimulus to distract you and derail your process. You allowed something to happen to you. That is the key. Own it!

Now, how can you fix your mental process to prevent it from happening again? After owning your mistake, then it would be appropriate to dig into why Two was out of position to begin with.

If you fail to take accountability for your mistakes, you are bound to repeat them. If something was not really your fault, then there is no need for you to do anything differently next time. There is no reason to grow; therefore, you will not grow. When you start explaining that your error is not your fault for some reason, we call that quibbling. Quibbling has no place in a fighter pilot debrief, and it will be called out. Quibbling is the fastest way to crush your credibility and your reputation. Your attitude is the only real threat in the debrief that should concern you.

The most effective flight leads and instructor pilots know the importance of leading this pursuit of personal accountability by example. When leading the debrief, it is critical that you go out of your way to make no attempt to hide any of your own mistakes. It would be so easy to do. When leading the debrief, you could purposefully not show portions of your tape where you knew you made an error. Would not that protect your credibility? Absolutely not! There is nothing less credible than someone who hides their mistakes while willingly pointing out the mistakes of others. No one wants to listen to that person.

Conversely, the best fighter pilots will go out of their way to show when they make a mistake, and they gain respect and credibility by doing so. This is not always easy to do, and God knows I have not always had the intestinal fortitude to go out of my way to highlight my mistakes. It is human nature to want to avoid accountability, but this is a counterproductive instinct. Your team will be so much more receptive to your feedback if you openly highlight your own errors so they can learn from them. It will disarm your team and communicate that this is a safe space. This is not about playing the blame game or an attack on their character; it is an attempt to improve as individuals and a team. You want to communicate that there is no need to worry about guarding your reputation in this space. Make your debrief most effective by never trying to minimize or disguise your mistakes when you are leading a debrief.

DEBRIEF STRUCTURE: PLAN, PRODUCT, BRIEF, ADMIN, TAC ADMIN, EXECUTION

Structure is necessary to get the most out of every debrief. Have you ever been in a "hot wash" that lacked structure? It is incredibly frustrating and chaotic. "Ok, we'll just open it up, and let's just see where the conversation takes us." In other words, "who knows if this meeting is worthwhile; I guess we will find out." Fighter pilots do not do this. There is a better way. When you provide a certain structure to a debrief, it organizes everything. It organizes people's thought processes and directs focus. If there is nothing of value in any focus area, then you move on to the next focus area. You are far less likely to miss key information in this type of format. Fighter pilots use a combination of categories and chronology to structure their debriefs.

Before any formal debrief starts, each fighter pilot does data gathering from their own tapes to "validate" all of their weapon releases and assess, "What did I do?" This is an attempt to get the "truth data" from their tapes, so when we reconstruct the fight, we can have the most accurate picture of what happened. There are times you may miss something in the air. For example, you took a shot and called a kill because it looked valid in the air, but after watching your tapes more closely, you missed a radar cue or bandit maneuvers that defeated your missile. We may have thought things went cleanly in the air, but that was not the case.

This is true with bomb drops as well. We may have thought we found and bombed the SAM radar that we wanted to, but upon tape review and comparing our target coordinates from the jet against the actual coordinates, we may find instead that we bombed a support vehicle. This would have significantly changed the fight and potentially caused additional Blue Force losses. It is vital that every individual knows exactly what they shot, when, and what the result is, so we can accurately reconstruct the fight as a group. Everyone shows up prepared. That is the expectation. Once the debrief starts, it will examine the plan, products, brief, admin, tactical admin, and then finally spend the bulk of the time on the execution.

Just like the brief, the debrief starts exactly on time with a recap of the mission objectives. This, once again, cages everyone around the focus of the debrief. Next, there is a fairly expeditious debrief of the basic plan for the mission. This allows the leader of the debrief to do a quick assessment of things he would change next time to enhance the scenario and make the training more efficient and effective. Because the plan will primarily be evaluated based on the debrief of the execution portion, I avoid making any conclusions about problems with the tactical plan during this time. The plan will be scrutinized much more thoroughly in the main execution debrief.

Next will be a quick debrief of any problems with the flying products. Was there any information missing that would have been helpful for execution? Were there any key contracts that were not clearly communicated on the card, or typos that could have been a factor in execution that were not caught in planning? Was there a better format for the information that could have been used to make it easier to reference in flight? This is a basic evaluation of the usefulness of the delivered products for execution. There are some sorties where this may be a significant debrief portion, but generally, this should be quick.

Debriefing the brief allows the leader the opportunity to acknowledge shortcomings in the communication of his tactical plan. If something were not clearly communicated, it would often come out in execution, so once again, this should be quick. It is reserved for the leader to highlight portions of the plan he realizes he failed to communicate effectively in the brief. This portion can sometimes be as simple as a question to the team: "Are there any questions from the brief?" The answer should almost always be "no." After all, the leader asked the same question at the end of his brief. If there were any questions, they should have been asked then. Nevertheless, sometimes people will realize they had a question much later and speak up at this time. In either case, the brief will continue to be evaluated throughout the execution debrief once we try to figure out what went wrong and why. That is when you find out if your brief failed to communicate important contracts.

The "goings and comings" admin debrief highlights problems in the administrative phases that could be fixed for next time. For instance, we would address if someone started to Taxi out of order and it caused confusion and delays for other assets. Perhaps that could even impact execution if it caused an asset to be late to the fight. If an aircraft emergency arose, how was it handled, and is there anything the group can learn from it? If there were a near mid-air in the traffic pattern, we would want to address that, as well.

The key here is identifying situations that could either have been a safety of flight issue or a potential impact on execution to fix them for next time. These are often considered boring items, but they could have massive consequences if not corrected. Fighter pilots do not like to talk about admin, but we know the importance of keeping it tight. Ideally, this is another truly short part of the debrief.

Debriefing tactical admin is like debriefing admin, but it is more focused on things that happened during execution that are significant. This would include things like Training Rule violations that were committed or observed during the fight. These are brought up immediately by the culprit. Training Rules exist to keep people safe. We have a common saying that "they are written in blood." Violations are serious and must be addressed immediately. While they are never intentional, that does not make them less unsafe. It is an extremely difficult profession, and mistakes happen. When they do, though, they must be addressed and corrected. Once again, there is no punishment to fear unless there is absolute gross negligence. When you leave the debrief, it is over, but all feedback must be addressed and taken very seriously. Additional tactical admin items are debriefed at this time, but once again, it should be quick. The idea is to get to the execution debrief with as much time as possible.

DEBRIEF FOCUS POINTS

Have you ever been in a debrief or "hot-wash" that lacked focus? I have, and it is frustrating. Fighter pilot debriefs are not that way. In addition to the chronological structure discussed in the previous chapter, there is also a structure for what to focus on and how to get the most out of that discussion. As we talked about previously, you want to value your team's time, and every debrief has limited time, so you need to make the most of it.

Identifying Debrief Focus Points (DFPs) are a great way to add structure and focus to your debrief. For fighter pilots, if you fail to meet your mission objective, that will drive a Debrief Focus Point. For instance, "Why did priority target Alpha go un-serviced, resulting in mission fail?" If one of your mission objectives is to have zero blue losses, then another Debrief Focus Point may be, "Why did number #4 die from 2X enemy missiles at 1423:25?" Simply put, you are selecting the most important things to look at first. DFPs are important and should take up the bulk of your allotted time. You may have several things that warrant a DFP. In that case, I usually work in chronological order. Any additional time remaining after addressing DFPs should be applied to Learning Points. Learning Points are significant items that you really want to address, but they do not quite rise to the level of compromising mission success. You certainly want to look at them for the team's benefit, but they are a lower priority. Finally, if there is any remaining time, it is at the leader's discretion to either give some time back to their team or address other interesting periods of the sortie that they can draw learning from.

After you clearly define the Debrief Focus Point to identify exactly what you want to address, you should identify anything that may have been a Contributing Factor (CF) for what went wrong. You are essentially creating an outline for your debrief using those potential Contributing Factors (CF). It is a good technique to always include the Plan and the Brief as potential contributing factors to be considered throughout the debrief process. Most fighter pilots adopt the technique of thinking through the analysis chronologically to help organize all the potential contributing factors that you can identify. Once you have your outline, you can start working through it logically.

Once you are systematically working through your DFP, you must debrief each potential contributing factor before moving on to the next one. The first question you need to answer is, "Was there an error made." If the answer is no, then you cross it off your list. During the analysis of your potential contributing factors, you may discover new potential contributing factors. As you identify new factors, you can add them to the list and evaluate them accordingly.

IDENTIFYING THE ERROR TYPE AND FIX

Before applying any instructional fix for an error, you must identify WHY the error was committed. To do this, fighter pilots first identify the type of error committed. Errors can be categorized into three types: **perception, decision,** and **execution.** Determining the type of error is a prerequisite to any fix. How can you accurately treat a problem if you fail to get the correct diagnosis? In the same way a good doctor finds the correct diagnosis before prescribing the proper medicine, you must diagnose the error before offering the correct fix. It is so easy to jump to conclusions as to why someone made an error. Questions are vital to teasing out the source of the error.

Consider an example where number Four is killed by an enemy aircraft that was targeting him. We want to examine his defensive response to see if there was an error committed and, if so, what type. If we watch Four's tape and determine he made no effort to execute a Defensive Response, I would need to ask questions to determine why. Those questions may sound like, "Did you recognize you were being targeted at abort range?" If he answers "no," then I have it. It is a **perception** issue.

Now we can find the root cause of why he failed to recognize he was being targeted. I may ask an open-ended question like, "At this time, what were you trying to do?" I do not ask why he failed to recognize he was targeted; I ask what he was doing instead. I likely already have an idea about the answer since I watched his tape, but I need confirmation. I also need buy-in. A perfect instructional fix is useless if the other person disagrees with you.

Perhaps I get the answer that "I was watching my radar countdown and focusing on calling a kill on the radio." I was likely already prepared for this answer, knowing he was making a radio call at that time, and this is a common mistake. Now, I know that the root cause was task mis-prioritization, leading to a breakdown in crosscheck. I was prepped for this possibility, but I needed confirmation. The instructional fix is simple but very difficult to execute.

"Next time, I will maintain a disciplined crosscheck, and approaching abort range, I will prioritize defensive response over Comm." Often in the debrief, you will receive an answer that you were not expecting. Therefore, it is important not to become anchored on any assumptions you had about what you think happened.

Now consider the same scenario. Only this time consider if he says "yes" to the question, "Did you recognize you were targeted at abort range?" In this case, I have some follow-up questions expecting this to most likely be a **decision** error, such as, "Why did you continue inside of abort range knowing you were targeted?" I may get a surprising answer like, "I thought that is what you briefed me to do based on the Acceptable Level of Risk (ALR) for the mission." If I get this answer, I need to revisit my brief as a likely contributing factor. Follow-on questions may sound like, "Do you remember from my brief what our ALR was?"

"Yes, it was high." If he answers correctly, I need to delve into his understanding of the Acceptable Level of Risk and what it means for a tactical intercept.

I may ask, "When are you able to defend yourself when we are under a "high" risk intercept? The root cause of his error may be as simple as a lack of understanding of tactics under different risk levels. That is an easy fix. Now, I just need to teach the correct actions on a tactical intercept under "high" risk criteria. A common misperception in fighter pilot students is to think that "high" risk means you are continuing no matter what, even though that is not the case. Clearing up this misunderstanding will fix his actions for next time. Next time, he will defend himself, and we will not have any blue losses.

Finally, consider the same scenario except, this time, Four did recognize that he was targeted at abort range and attempted to execute an abort. However, he was still killed despite his abort maneuver. Now when we watch the tapes, we recognize that his abort was "weak," meaning that it was not as aggressive as it needed to be. He failed to meet the assumptions that abort range was built on and, as a result, was still vulnerable to the kinematics of the enemy missile. In this case, I still want to ask some questions. We know the "what," but we still need to know the "why."

I am looking for all the same things with my questioning. I want to know if he was distracted by something else, if he did not understand the correct way to execute an abort, or if he simply could not make the jet do what he wanted it to do. Maybe he knew what he wanted to do, but he just could not make the jet execute. Easy, this is an **execution** error. Now, I can use my knowledge and expertise to provide an instructional fix for the power and flight control inputs necessary to do it next time under similar conditions.

I may get a common answer like, "I don't know" or, "I was behind the jet and didn't know what to do." The "I don't know" answer is prevalent among students. Things are happening so quickly that even though they know what to do, they simply freeze or get behind the jet and react too late. It is the job of the experienced instructor to help them understand the why. At this point, the line blurs between perception, decision, and execution errors. Sometimes they are all involved, but it is important to find the root cause of why he got behind the jet or froze.

These are complex situations that take time and deliberate attention to diagnose. It is not always easy, but it is incredibly important. Trying to fix all three simultaneously will prove cumbersome and likely lead to confusion. Remember, the purpose of the debrief is to learn and get better, not assign blame or find every single mistake. Focus on the most important things that can make the team more elite.

After analyzing each potential contributing factor, fighter pilots like to choose a "primary contributing factor." This allows fighter pilots to identify the most important factor that caused the DFP. Identifying the most important factor allows fighter pilots to spend a little extra time emphasizing its importance for the entire group. Ideally, your team can internalize and fix every contributing factor for next time, but that is likely unrealistic. If they take anything away, the primary contributing factor is the most important. Everyone must understand the root cause of this error. For, if you can fix it for next time, the mission will succeed.

THREE KEY TAKEAWAYS

Debriefs can be overwhelming at times. There is so much learning you can delve into and squeeze out of one debrief that it is possible to leave with information overload. This is not entirely a bad thing, but the number of things you need to fix could be too much all at once. You need to eat that elephant one bite at a time, and you want those next bites to be the most critical ones for your team's success.

One technique that fighter pilot instructors widely adopt is to boil the debrief down into three key takeaways. If your team gets nothing else from the debrief, you want them to walk away with this. In a way, it serves as a summary to focus your team. For the entirety of this book, I have utilized a summary section at the end that uses a version of this technique. That is really what you are doing. You want to summarize the debrief by offering three things that your team can focus on for next time. This can take some thought and effort to "dilute" your debrief to just the basics, but it is worth your time. If you are stuck with just two or want to expand it to four, that is just fine. It is a tool, not a rule.

Finally, before closing out every debrief, fighter pilots grade their team's execution against the Mission Objectives and Tactical Objectives. This, once again, brings attention back to the big picture. What were we trying to do today, and how did we measure up? We had an objective;

did we achieve it? We grade it with a simple + or –, but it helps re-cage everyone back from the nitty-gritty details of the mission to the team's overall performance. Even if there are a bunch of – marks on the board, we now know how to turn them all +. Do not get bogged down in the details. Details are important, but you do not want to miss the forest for the trees.

Debriefing is an art that is more effective when a repeatable structure exists to guide and focus the debrief. The overarching goal is always growth, and therefore personal accountability is paramount, and you should lead by example. A repeatable structure will allow you to expeditiously cover necessary administrative concerns while saving the bulk of your debriefing time for what is most important. Debrief focus points add structure to your debrief and enable more in-depth error analysis. When you can correctly identify what happened and why it happened, you can provide an appropriate instructional fix that will help you and your team continuously improve!

SUMMARY FOR APPLICATION

1. **Personal accountability is paramount:** The purpose of the debrief is to get better for next time—not to assign blame. However, sugar coating errors or glossing over them will squander your opportunity to improve. Understand and acknowledge the reasons, but do not make excuses. The leader must lead by example and set the tone for the debrief by owning mistakes.

2. **Structure your debrief to maximize learning:** Structure your debrief to efficiently get into the most important topics without getting bogged down in minute details. Try to get to the execution portion of your debrief as quickly as possible while still addressing necessary administrative issues. This will make your debrief more effective and efficient.

3. **Identify Contributing Factors, identify the error, and provide a fix:** Identify errors that may have contributed to your Debrief Focus

Point. Was it a perception, decision, or execution error, and what was the root cause for why it was committed? Only once these are determined can you provide the correct fix.

LASTING IMPACT

THE UNITED STATES PRODUCES the world's greatest fighter pilots because of the culture and process practiced by its people. To be successful flying fighter jets, especially in the modern world, a person must be constantly improving. The fighter pilot's path to elite performance is through rapid growth made possible by certain values, attitudes, and processes.

In Part 1 of this book, we examined the values and attitudes that drive fighter pilots to be trustworthy, high performers with incredibly high potential for growth. If you can unleash human potential to grow, it is remarkable what human beings are capable of. I am convinced that there is a rare culture amongst American fighter pilots that harnesses human growth potential. That is one of the reasons I decided to write this book. It starts with embracing the core values of integrity, service, and excellence. These core values manifest themselves in a culture that treasures personal accountability and taking responsibility for your actions. These values can create communities that idealize the humble, approachable, and credible. This inevitably produces a culture that can be aggressive and competitive while maintaining a team mentality that works together for the ultimate cause of achieving our objectives to maintain safety and security for the American people.

In Part 2 of this book, we took a careful look at the process fighter pilots use to achieve mission success and continue to grow. The intent was not only to highlight the steps that lead to a successful mission but, more importantly, to show how every value and character trait we talked about in Part 1 influences every step in the process. Aggregating an extensive and complex set of information to develop a cohesive plan takes incredible teamwork, discipline, and desire. Clearly communicating the plan in the brief takes confidence and excellence. Execution requires trust, flexibility, confidence, and aggressiveness that is practiced daily. We even discussed how fighter pilots approach emergency situations and the importance of remaining calm, confident, and competent to handle the situation. Finally, the debrief is where humility, personal accountability, and a commitment to excellence are most clearly needed to grow the fighter pilot. It is all about the growth of the people. For our mission to succeed, we must continue to produce increasingly more competent fighter pilots. There must be growth.

As my career as a fighter pilot came to an end, I spent more time considering my legacy. Has my service made a difference in the world for good? I have had this career that I am proud of, but what is the long-term impact I am leaving behind? I had considered these questions during my time as a fighter pilot, but they felt far more pressing as I left my last fighter squadron for the final time. Often, we need to reach the end of something to find more clarity on our purpose. Nothing forces reflection like an ending. Unfortunately, at the end it is too late to change course and pursue your purpose with intention. I believe living intentionally is aided by an eternal perspective that is lived out day by day.

Long after the fighter jets that I flew are decommissioned and rusted, the people I was able to influence will continue to live on. I am convinced that people will live on in eternity, and that should have very profound implications on how we treat each other. Yes, I am proud of the things I accomplished in my career. However, I think more about what will have lasting impacts. I do believe the safety and security that I helped secure for the American people as a member of the armed forces has real, long-lasting impacts. I am proud I was able to help contribute to this mission. However, as I leave the military, I consider the people I leave behind more important.

What impact did I have on their growth? I am proud of the men and women I served with and feel secure knowing they are safeguarding America's freedom moving forward. I watched young wingmen develop into outstanding instructors and leaders whose capabilities well exceed my own. Our fighter pilots have what it takes to win. That gives me some lasting comfort. However, the purpose I want to pursue is not simply to add competency, but to add value to the personal lives of those I must one day leave behind.

I believe perhaps the most direct and long-lasting impact any person can have is in the individual lives of the people they touch. How did I treat people? Are they better off for having known me? Did I help them grow as a person? Every interaction and every investment in someone's life has meaning. Perhaps more profound and eternal meaning than anything we might ever "achieve" in our lifetime. Life is not primarily about jets or industries or equipment or companies. It is all about people. Investing in people pays dividends. Both today and, potentially, into eternity.

ACKNOWLEDGMENTS

In writing this book, I drew from lessons and experiences from my Air Force career. I benefited from many outstanding leaders, instructors, students, and peers who taught me how to grow and win. To them, I am forever grateful and proud to have served along such incredible men and women. Thank you to the friends and family who encouraged me and provided helpful input to make this book more appealing and impactful. To my editors, thank you for your diligence in correcting errors and filtering out distractions to make this book more focused and readable. Finally, thank you to my wonderful wife for your unending love and support.

ABOUT THE AUTHOR

Major (retired) Paul "HAZE" Gannett served as an officer in the United States Air Force upon graduation from the Air Force Academy in Colorado Springs, Colorado. Paul earned his wings from the Euro-NATO Joint Jet Pilot Training program and was selected to fly the F-15E "Strike Eagle." Later in his career, he transitioned to the F-35 as an instructor. In total, "HAZE" amassed over 1500 flight hours in fighter aircraft including more than 400 in combat. His Air Force career ended in medical retirement after over 11 years of active duty service. He now serves as a wealth advisor at Pinkerton Retirement Specialists, LLC.

www.ingramcontent.com/pod-product-compliance
Lightning Source LLC
Chambersburg PA
CBHW051100250726

48656CB00001B/401